Christ Crucified

New Testament Theology

Edited by Thomas R. Schreiner and Brian S. Rosner

The Beginning of the Gospel: A Theology of Mark, Peter Orr

From the Manger to the Throne: A Theology of Luke, Benjamin L. Gladd

The Mission of the Triune God: A Theology of Acts, Patrick Schreiner

Ministry in the New Realm: A Theology of 2 Corinthians, Dane C. Ortlund

Christ Crucified: A Theology of Galatians, Thomas R. Schreiner

United to Christ, Walking in the Spirit: A Theology of Ephesians, Benjamin L. Merkle

Hidden with Christ in God: A Theology of Colossians and Philemon, Kevin W. McFadden

To Walk and to Please God: A Theology of 1 and 2 Thessalonians, Andrew S. Malone

Perfect Priest for Weary Pilgrims: A Theology of Hebrew, Dennis E. Johnson

The God Who Judges and Saves: A Theology of 2 Peter and Jude, Matthew S. Harmon

The Joy of Hearing: A Theology of the Book of Revelation, Thomas R. Schreiner

"Tom Schreiner is a treasure of the contemporary church. He has written commentaries and other scholarly material that have rightly earned accolades. And this current volume rises to the very top. How I wish I had this book when I preached through Galatians over a decade ago. It fills a significant need: a book that gives you the overall theology of Galatians. Every preacher has experienced the moment when you end a sermon series on a book of the Bible only to realize that you are now in a much better place to start all over again! Typically, a commentary introduction might attempt to address the overall theology of a particular book, but we need far more. *Christ Crucified* provides just that."

    Derek W. H. Thomas, Chancellor's Professor of Systematic and
    Pastoral Theology, Reformed Theological Seminary; Teaching Fellow,
    Ligonier Ministries

"When Christ ascended to the Father's right hand, he gave gifts to the church, including teachers and pastors. We can be thankful that Tom Schreiner is among those gifts to the church. He ably and accessibly teaches readers about the key themes of Paul's epistle to the Galatians. *Christ Crucified* is a valuable resource for anyone who wants a deeper knowledge of the gospel of Christ."

    J. V. Fesko, Harriet Barbour Professor of Systematic and Historical
    Theology, Reformed Theological Seminary, Jackson

"*Christ Crucified* provides a clear, thorough, and knowledgeable introduction to the theology of Galatians. In it, Tom Schreiner leads the reader through every major theological theme in the letter, interacting irenically and thoughtfully with other interpreters and coming to reasonable, pastorally helpful conclusions. This is just the kind of concise, reliable introduction to the letter that students, pastors, and teachers will find helpful in their studies and in preparing to preach and teach this theologically powerful biblical text."

    Frank Thielman, Presbyterian Chair of Divinity, Beeson Divinity School

Christ Crucified

A Theology of Galatians

Thomas R. Schreiner

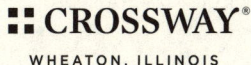

WHEATON, ILLINOIS

Christ Crucified: A Theology of Galatians
© 2024 by Thomas R. Schreiner
Published by Crossway
    1300 Crescent Street
    Wheaton, Illinois 60187

All rights reserved. No part of this publication may be reproduced, stored in a retrieval system, or transmitted in any form by any means, electronic, mechanical, photocopy, recording, or otherwise, without the prior permission of the publisher, except as provided for by USA copyright law. Crossway® is a registered trademark in the United States of America.

Cover design: Jordan Singer

First printing 2024

Printed in the United States of America

Unless otherwise indicated, Scripture quotations are from the ESV® Bible (The Holy Bible, English Standard Version®), © 2001 by Crossway, a publishing ministry of Good News Publishers. Used by permission. All rights reserved. The ESV text may not be quoted in any publication made available to the public by a Creative Commons license. The ESV may not be translated in whole or in part into any other language.

Scripture quotations marked CSB have been taken from the Christian Standard Bible®, copyright © 2017 by Holman Bible Publishers. Used by permission. Christian Standard Bible® and CSB® are federally registered trademarks of Holman Bible Publishers.

Scripture quotations marked KJV are from the King James Version of the Bible. Public domain.

Scripture quotations marked NASB 1995 are taken from the New American Standard Bible®, copyright © 1960, 1971, 1977, 1995 by The Lockman Foundation. Used by permission. All rights reserved. www.lockman.org.

Scripture quotations designated NET are from the NET Bible® copyright © 1996–2016 by Biblical Studies Press, L.L.C. http://netbible.com. Used by permission. All rights reserved.

Scripture quotations marked NIV are taken from the Holy Bible, New International Version®, NIV®. Copyright © 1973, 1978, 1984, 2011 by Biblica, Inc.™ Used by permission of Zondervan. All rights reserved worldwide. www.zondervan.com. The "NIV" and "New International Version" are trademarks registered in the United States Patent and Trademark Office by Biblica, Inc.™

Scripture quotations marked NRSV are from the New Revised Standard Version Bible, copyright © 1989 the Division of Christian Education of the National Council of the Churches of Christ in the United States of America. Used by permission. All rights reserved.

Scripture quotations marked RSV are from the Revised Standard Version of the Bible, copyright © 1946, 1952, and 1971 the Division of Christian Education of the National Council of the Churches of Christ in the United States of America. Used by permission. All rights reserved.

All emphases in Scripture quotations have been added by the author.

Trade paperback ISBN: 978-1-4335-8130-4
ePub ISBN: 978-1-4335-8132-8
PDF ISBN: 978-1-4335-8131-1

Library of Congress Cataloging-in-Publication Data

Names: Schreiner, Thomas R., author.
Title: Christ crucified : a theology of Galatians / Thomas R. Schreiner.
Description: Wheaton, Illinois : Crossway, 2024. | Series: New Testament theology | Includes bibliographical references and index.
Identifiers: LCCN 2024000063 | ISBN 9781433581304 (trade paperback) | ISBN 9781433581311 (pdf) | ISBN 9781433581328 (epub)
Subjects: LCSH: Bible. Galatians—Criticism, interpretation, etc.
Classification: LCC BS2685.2 .S34 2024 | DDC 227/.406—dc23/eng/20240304
LC record available at https://lccn.loc.gov/2024000063

Crossway is a publishing ministry of Good News Publishers.

VP		33	32	31	30	29	28	27	26	25	24
15	14	13	12	11	10	9	8	7	6	5	4	3	2	1

Contents

Series Preface *ix*
Preface *xi*
Abbreviations *xiii*

Part 1
THE CONFLICT

1 The Adversaries *3*
2 Paul's Apostolic Authority *15*

Part 2
THE GOSPEL

3 Eschatology and Apocalyptic *31*
4 Circumcision and the Cross *47*
5 Justification by Faith *57*
6 The Law *75*

Part 3
THE NEW LIFE

7 The Family of Abraham *97*
8 Life in the Spirit *111*

Epilogue *123*
Appendix: A Review of *Paul and the Gift* by John M. G. Barclay *125*

Recommended Resources *137*

General Index *145*

Scripture and Ancient Sources Index *151*

Series Preface

There are remarkably few treatments of the big ideas of single books of the New Testament. Readers can find brief coverage in Bible dictionaries, in some commentaries, and in New Testament theologies, but such books are filled with other information and are not devoted to unpacking the theology of each New Testament book in its own right. Technical works concentrating on various themes of New Testament theology often have a narrow focus, treating some aspect of the teaching of, say, Matthew or Hebrews in isolation from the rest of the book's theology.

The New Testament Theology series seeks to fill this gap by providing students of Scripture with readable book-length treatments of the distinctive teaching of each New Testament book or collection of books. The volumes approach the text from the perspective of biblical theology. They pay due attention to the historical and literary dimensions of the text, but their main focus is on presenting the teaching of particular New Testament books about God and his relations to the world on their own terms, maintaining sight of the Bible's overarching narrative and Christocentric focus. Such biblical theology is of fundamental importance to biblical and expository preaching and informs exegesis, systematic theology, and Christian ethics.

The twenty volumes in the series supply comprehensive, scholarly, and accessible treatments of theological themes from an evangelical perspective. We envision them being of value to students, preachers, and interested laypeople. When preparing an expository sermon series, for example, pastors can find a healthy supply of informative commentaries, but there are few options for coming to terms with the overall teaching of each book of the New Testament. As well as being useful in sermon and Bible study preparation, the volumes will also be of value as textbooks in college and seminary exegesis classes. Our prayer is that they contribute to a deeper understanding of and commitment to the kingdom and glory of God in Christ.

Written in response to a serious crisis in the church, Galatians is Paul's most passionate and strident letter. Schreiner's theology of Galatians provides a vivid portrait of Paul's opponents and locates the crux of the dispute in an understanding of the cross. Christ crucified not only spells the end of the old age and the inauguration of the new but also provides a new understanding of covenant, law, the family of Abraham, God's work of deliverance, and the new creation. Schreiner provides a lucid and compelling exposition of Paul's gospel, presenting the good news of our full and free acceptance with God, freedom in Christ, and new life in the Spirit.

Thomas R. Schreiner and Brian S. Rosner

Preface

As one of the coeditors of the series, I wasn't planning on writing more than one volume since I had already written on the book of Revelation. But as everyone who edits a series knows, sometimes contributors who are slated to write particular volumes have to drop out for various reasons. Even then I didn't seriously consider writing this book; but I received encouragement to do so, and my love for Galatians won out. I have previously written a commentary on the letter, and I suppose (even from my doctoral days) that Galatians is the letter I invested the most time in. Thus, it was a special delight to return to it again.

As I reflected on how to outline the book, my son Patrick was a particular help as I bounced ideas off him about how to structure my presentation. The theme pursued in this book is the truth of the gospel, a phrase Paul uses twice in the letter (Gal. 2:5, 14). I divided the volume into three parts because there is a natural progression in the book. In part 1, we have the conflict between Paul and the opponents that must be resolved. The adversaries (chap. 1) questioned Paul's apostolic authority and his gospel, and thus (chap. 2) Paul must defend his apostolic authority in order to defend the gospel. The gospel is bound up with Paul's apostolic ministry so that in this case they can't be split apart.

Part 2 examines the gospel itself. It is the truth of this gospel that Paul defends over against the opponents. Under eschatology and apocalyptic (chap. 3), I explore the fulfillment theme in the letter and explain that Paul's gospel is both eschatological and apocalyptic, which is a current debate in Pauline studies. The newness of God's work in Christ—that is, the end of the old age and the inauguration of the new—is sketched in here. Chapter 4 centers on Christ and the cross (but includes the resurrection as well). Here I show that the cross is at the center of Paul's gospel and of history and that the cross—not circumcision—is necessary for entrance into the people of God in the new era that has dawned. Either one accepts Christ crucified as the path to salvation or turns to the law and to human performance. Chapter 5 considers further the implications of the Christ event and the cross being the center of history. We see that a right understanding of the cross indicates that justification is by faith alone. The Reformation understanding of justification doesn't misread the New Testament but accurately captures the message of Paul in Galatians. The newness that has come about in Christ provokes questions about the law, and I explore in chapter 6 what Paul says about the law and what it means for our understanding of covenant.

Then in part 3, we see what it looks like to live out the truth of the gospel in the new era. Chapter 7 considers the people of God, what I am calling the family of Abraham. The boundaries of God's people are redrawn through Jesus Christ, and thus Jews and Gentiles are one in Christ Jesus. Old tribalisms and ethnocentrism are set aside in the family of God. Then in the final chapter, I explore the new life of the Spirit, showing that the Spirit is the engine for the Christian life, that believers who are indwelt by the Spirit live transformed lives. The book concludes with a short epilogue, summing up the path the book has traversed.

This book was stimulated in part by an invitation to give lectures at Moore Theological College, and I am thankful for the invitation and the opportunity to share my study. I also want to thank Justin Taylor, executive vice president of book publishing for Crossway, for encouraging me to write the book. I am also grateful for Chris Cowan who was—a long time ago and far away—one of my PhD students but who now has served as an editor for several books that I have written. Chris's light touch as an editor and his keen eye have helped me immensely, and I am thankful for his suggestions that have made the book better than it would have been otherwise.

Abbreviations

AB	Anchor Bible
Ant.	*Jewish Antiquities*, by Josephus
2 Bar.	2 Baruch
BBR	*Bulletin for Biblical Research*
BECNT	Baker Exegetical Commentary on the New Testament
Bib	*Biblica*
BJRL	*Bulletin of the John Ryland University Library of Manchester*
BNTC	Black's New Testament Commentary
BZNW	Beihefte zur Zeitschrift für die neutestamentliche Wissenschaft
CBQ	*Catholic Biblical Quarterly*
CC	Continental Commentaries
CD	Damascus Document
ConcC	Concordia Commentary
CSC	Christian Standard Commentary
CTJ	*Calvin Theological Journal*
1 En.	1 Enoch
ExpTim	*Expository Times*
HTR	*Harvard Theological Review*
ICC	International Critical Commentary
IVPNTC	IVP New Testament Commentary
JBL	*Journal of Biblical Literature*

JETS	*Journal of the Evangelical Theological Society*
JSJ	*Journal for the Study of Judaism in the Persian, Hellenistic, and Roman Periods*
JSNT	*Journal for the Study of the New Testament*
JSNTSup	Journal for the Study of the New Testament Supplement Series
JTS	*Journal of Theological Studies*
Jub.	Jubilees
LNTS	The Library of New Testament Studies
LXX	Septuagint
m. 'Abot	'Abot (Mishnah)
1–4 Macc.	1–4 Maccabees
Migr.	*On the Migration of Abraham*, by Philo
MT	Masoretic Text
NCC	New Covenant Commentary
NICNT	New International Commentary on the New Testament
NICOT	New International Commentary on the Old Testament
NIGTC	New International Greek Testament Commentary
NIVAC	NIV Application Commentary
NovT	*Novum Testamentum*
NSBT	New Studies in Biblical Theology
NTL	New Testament Library
NTS	*New Testament Studies*
OTP	Old Testament Pseudepigrapha. Edited by James H. Charlesworth. 2 vols. New York: Doubleday, 1983, 1985.
Pss. Sol.	Psalms of Solomon
1QpHab	Pesher Habakkuk
4QpNah	Pesher Nahum
11QTemple	Temple Scroll
Sir.	Sirach
SNTSMS	Society for New Testament Studies Monograph Series

SP	Sacra Pagina
Spec. Laws	*On the Special Laws*, by Philo
SSST	Short Studies in Systematic Theology
TDNT	*Theological Dictionary of the New Testament*. Edited by Gerhard Kittel and Gerhard Friedrich. Translated by Geoffrey W. Bromiley. 10 vols. Grand Rapids, MI: Eerdmas, 1964–76.
Them	*Themelios*
TynBul	*Tyndale Bulletin*
WBC	Word Biblical Commentary
WTJ	*Westminster Theological Journal*
WUNT	Wissenschaftliche Untersuchungen zum Neuen Testament
ZECNT	Zondervan Exegetical Commentary on the New Testament

PART 1
———

THE CONFLICT

1

The Adversaries

Introduction

Galatians heralds the truth of the gospel, and this gospel stands as the authority over all people everywhere. Thus, Paul defends it passionately in the letter (Gal. 2:5, 14) over against his antagonists. The adversaries in Galatia, on the other hand, insisted that Paul deviated from the gospel and that he wasn't a genuine apostle. The identity of the opponents in Galatians has been a matter of sharp controversy over the years, and examining that issue in detail would require a longer chapter than is possible here.[1] Instead I will attempt to paint a portrait of the agitators from the letter itself. Such an enterprise is not without risks since we don't hear the adversaries in their own voice. We only know about their views through what Paul says about them. If we could talk to Paul's opponents, we would certainly gain a fuller and deeper understanding of their perspective. Since we are confined to what Paul says about the agitators and since Paul doesn't provide a full account of their views, we have to engage in what is called mirror reading.[2] From what Paul writes, we attempt to discern the identity and theology of the opponents. We recognize our historical distance from the first readers at

---

1 For a more detailed discussion on the identity of the opponents, see Thomas R. Schreiner, *Galatians*, ZECNT (Grand Rapids, MI: Zondervan, 2010), 31–52.
2 The classic essay on this is John M. G. Barclay, "Mirror-Reading a Polemical Letter: Galatians as a Test Case," *JSNT* 31 (1987): 73–93.

this very point since the Galatians knew who the adversaries were and what they taught. Paul assumes such knowledge in writing the letter to the Galatians, reminding us that the letter wasn't written to us but to the first readers.[3]

Paul gives us enough information in Galatians so that we can sketch in quite a full picture of those who resisted him. For those of us who believe in divine inspiration of the Scriptures, we also believe that God has given us all the information we need to understand the letter. The providence of God is such that what we have in the Scriptures is sufficient to understand their message. In the case of Galatians we don't claim to have a comprehensive grasp of the letter as if everything is perfectly clear. But I do claim that enough information is given so that we have a clear understanding of the central message of the letter.

We don't enjoy absolute certainty about the identity of the opposition, but they bear striking similarities to the Pharisees who debated with Paul and Barnabas in Acts 15. Even if they were not the same people, they shared the same perspective on the law, the law that was given on Mount Sinai. These Pharisaic believers in Christ insisted that Gentile believers should get circumcised and keep the Mosaic law and that such was necessary for salvation (Acts 15:1, 5). The Galatian agitators almost certainly advanced the same argument, as we shall see. It is probable as well that those troubling the Galatians came from outside the church. Thus, it is possible that the opponents hailed from Jerusalem or possibly Syrian Antioch. If that is the case, they traveled to Galatia, declaring the same message that they promulgated in Israel and its near environs. We don't know, of course, whether Paul's opponents were the same people who questioned him and Barnabas in Acts 15. What does seem plausible, however, is that—if they were distinct from those in Jerusalem and Syrian Antioch—they advocated the same message.

---

3   Incidentally I support a south Galatian destination of the letter and an early dating as well (see Schreiner, *Galatians*, 22–31), but no major interpretation depends on this historical reconstruction.

Questioned Paul's Apostolic Authority

As we examine Galatians, some features of the adversaries' teaching come into sharper focus. For instance, we have good reasons to think that they questioned Paul's apostolic authority, and this is particularly evident in Galatians 1–2. We have a hint that they had doubts about Paul from the outset of the letter since in the first verse, after declaring that he was an apostle, Paul immediately adds that he was "not from men nor through man" (Gal. 1:1). Paul often begins his letters by asserting that he was an apostle (Rom. 1:1; 1 Cor. 1:1; 2 Cor. 1:1; Eph. 1:1; Col. 1:1; 1 Tim. 1:1; 2 Tim. 1:1; Titus 1:1), but this is the only letter where he immediately claims that his apostleship didn't have a human source. A note of self-defense, an apology of Paul's apostolic legitimacy, peeks through the first verse of the letter! Paul defended himself from the beginning because the opponents questioned his apostolic authority. The agitators likely claimed that Paul failed to tell the Galatians that they had to be circumcised (more on this shortly) because he wanted to please people (Gal. 1:10). Perhaps they even claimed that Paul preached circumcision elsewhere (Gal. 5:11) and that he failed to bring up the matter in Galatia because he didn't want to offend them.

Our historical distance from Galatians may screen us from the distinctiveness of Paul's apostolic ministry. We need to remember that Paul wasn't one of the original twelve apostles who were commissioned by Jesus and who accompanied him throughout his ministry. Paul himself says that he was "untimely born" (*ektrōma*) and confesses he was "unworthy" to be an apostle since he persecuted the church (1 Cor. 15:8–9; cf. 1 Tim. 1:12–16). We don't know if Paul ever met Jesus while he was on earth. One can easily understand, then, that questions could be raised about Paul's apostolic legitimacy. We can imagine the opponents saying to the Galatians, "Who is this person who never walked and talked with Jesus? Where did he get his gospel? And does it agree with the gospel proclaimed by the apostles in Jerusalem?" In other words, they probably claimed that Paul's gospel was *dependent* on the apostles from Jerusalem and that he *distorted* what the twelve taught.[4] They could have unsettled the Galatians by saying that the gospel Paul taught was not the same gospel that the twelve taught in Jerusalem. Paul's gospel was an outlier, they charged, not in accord with the gospel proclaimed elsewhere in the world.

The adversaries asserted, then, that Paul's gospel was human and not from God or Jesus Christ (Gal. 1:11). I should note, by the way, that we have no clear evidence that these agitators denied that Jesus was the Messiah. Apparently, there was no argument on that matter, and thus both Paul and the opponents claimed that they were Christians—followers of Christ. If they denied that Jesus was the Messiah or that he had risen from the dead, we can be sure that Paul would have responded vigorously. Despite their common belief that Jesus was the Messiah, these troublemakers (1:7; 5:10) asserted that Paul didn't proclaim the true gospel, the gospel that emanated from Jerusalem, the gospel preached by the twelve apostles. Paul's so-called gospel, according to his antagonists, was transmitted to him by human beings and didn't have a divine origin (1:12).

Demanded Observance of Circumcision and the Law

We have seen that the opponents in Galatia questioned Paul's apostolic authority, asserting that his gospel was merely human since it did not agree with the Jerusalem apostles. But what was the controversy between Paul and the agitators precisely? What was the issue that led to such a fierce dispute? If we work backwards and consult the end of the letter, the difference between Paul and the antagonists surfaces, and it comes out most clearly in Galatians 6:12–13

> It is those who want to make a good showing in the flesh who would force you to be circumcised, and only in order that they may not be persecuted for the cross of Christ. For even those who are circum-

---

4   The use of the word *twelve* here should not be understood technically, as if there were only twelve apostles. It stands for the apostolic circle in Jerusalem and stems from Jesus's appointment of twelve apostles in his ministry.

cised do not themselves keep the law, but they desire to have you circumcised that they may boast in your flesh.

Paul's accusations against his adversaries aren't my concern here; what we see without any doubt is that the opponents required circumcision, that they reproved the Galatians for failing to observe this command from the torah. We have another indication that the issue was circumcision in Galatians 5:2–4 since Paul warns the Galatians in the strongest possible way about the fatal consequences that will follow if they get circumcised. They are warned that they will be severed from Christ, fall from grace, and face eschatological judgment if they receive circumcision. Paul also tells the story in Galatians 2:3–5 about some "false brothers" who wanted to impose circumcision on Titus when he traveled to Jerusalem with Paul and Barnabas. Actually, if we are reading Galatians for the very first time, we don't realize as we encounter this story about the conflict over circumcision in Jerusalem that circumcision was also controversial in Galatia. After reading the entire letter, however, we understand why Paul brought up the story of the attempt to get Titus circumcised. He foreshadows in Galatians 2 the debate that was raging in the Galatian churches.

For modern readers the claim that one must be circumcised seems strange and perhaps even bizarre, but when we read the Old Testament the demand of the opponents has much more credibility. They almost certainly appealed to Genesis 17:9–14:

> And God said to Abraham, "As for you, you shall keep my covenant, you and your offspring after you throughout their generations. This is my covenant, which you shall keep, between me and you and your offspring after you: Every male among you shall be circumcised. You shall be circumcised in the flesh of your foreskins, and it shall be a sign of the covenant between me and you. He who is eight days old among you shall be circumcised. Every male throughout your generations, whether born in your house or bought with your money from any foreigner who is not of your offspring, both he who is born

in your house and he who is bought with your money, shall surely be circumcised. So shall my covenant be in your flesh an everlasting covenant. Any uncircumcised male who is not circumcised in the flesh of his foreskin shall be cut off from his people; he has broken my covenant."

Several features of these verses were probably trumpeted by the adversaries. (1) The covenant is to be observed "throughout their generations" for Abraham's "offspring after you" (Gen. 17:9) so that the covenant is "everlasting" (17:13). The agitators surely claimed that there was no evidence that circumcision was obsolete. The Bible says it must be kept forever! (2) The covenant is universal and there are no exceptions: "every male among you shall be circumcised" (Gen. 17:10), "every male throughout your generations" (17:12), including all foreigners (that means Gentiles!) (17:12–13), and "any uncircumcised male" (17:14). (3) Circumcision is required as the covenant sign and thus must be kept. The word "covenant" is used six times in this short paragraph, showing how important circumcision was. Those who refuse to be circumcised are "cut off" (Gen 17:14; the pun is deliberate) from God's covenant—they are not part of the people of God. It isn't so surprising, then, that the Pharisaic believers in Acts 15:1 said that circumcision was required to be saved, and the Galatian agitators almost certainly said the same thing. Those who aren't circumcised, they claimed, are severed from God himself and from his covenant with his people. (4) Finally, circumcision isn't merely spiritual but is also physical. Circumcision is "in the flesh of your foreskins" (Gen. 17:11); and in case we misunderstand, it is repeated—each one must "be circumcised in the flesh of his foreskin" (17:14). It would not do, the opponents must have said, to restrict circumcision to a spiritual matter since it is patently clear that circumcision was physical, involving the removal of the foreskin.

When we read the Old Testament and grasp the nature of the Lord's covenant with Israel, we understand why circumcision was considered to be indispensable by Paul's adversaries. Controversies don't typically exist if the other side doesn't have some plausible things to say. When we examine the Old Testament the necessity of circumcision is impressed on us. I have already noted the strong words in Genesis 17:9–14. In addition, every Hebrew boy was to be circumcised after his birth on the eighth day (Lev. 12:3; cf. Jub. 15:12), and we know from Philippians 3:5 that Paul's parents had him circumcised on the eighth day as well. A remarkable story about Israel entering the land of promise is found in Joshua 5:2–9. We discover that the children of the wilderness generation weren't circumcised, and before they were allowed to enter the land of promise they had to be circumcised. We learn from this that the covenant people could not receive the covenant promise of the land without the covenant sign being applied to their bodies. The covenantal significance of circumcision also explains the bizarre story about Yahweh threatening to kill Moses as he was returning to Egypt as God's deliverer, as the mediator of the Lord's liberation of Israel from Egyptian slavery (Ex. 4:24–26). The meaning of the passage is intensely debated, and thus there is only space here to present my own reading. Why would Yahweh try to kill Moses? We see that his death is only averted when Zipporah circumcises her son, calling Moses a "bridegroom of blood" as she touches Moses's feet with her son's foreskin. Probably Zipporah resisted circumcising her children since it wasn't the custom of her clan. But the covenant deliverer (Moses) could not return to Egypt and save Israel if the covenant sign was flouted in his very own family. The account impresses on us that circumcision wasn't an optional choice to belong to Israel. The Lord demanded it from his people.

The post-Old Testament history of Israel also confirms the importance of circumcision. Circumcision became the center of controversy when Antiochus Epiphanes—a Seleucid king—exercised control over Israel (ruled 175–164 BC). Antiochus wanted to turn Israel's cult into one that accorded with his own pagan culture (1 Macc. 1:41–50), and thus he suppressed Jewish customs and oppressed those insisting on observing the torah. Some Jews compromised and even "removed the marks of circumcision" (1 Macc. 1:15 NRSV) since death was decreed for those who violated the king's command. On the other hand, mothers, families, and children who were circumcised were even put to death (1 Macc. 1:60–61; 2 Macc. 6:10; 4 Macc. 4:25) for their allegiance to the law and to God's covenant. Israelites were viciously persecuted for observing the torah. We can understand why some in Israel would be outraged, therefore, when Paul diminished the importance of circumcision since about two hundred years earlier Jews had lost their lives for their faithfulness to the Lord's commands.

The importance of circumcision wasn't lessened during the Second Temple period (roughly 400 BC–AD 200). Circumcision is considered to be an "eternal ordinance" in Jubilees (15:25 *OTP*),[5] and those who aren't circumcised "on the eighth day" have "broken" the Lord's covenant and will "be destroyed and annihilated from the earth" (Jub. 15:26 *OTP*). Reading Josephus confirms that circumcision continued to be understood in Paul's day as a physical requirement for covenant membership (*Ant.* 1:192 [1.10.5]). Alternatively, some have said that circumcision wasn't necessary for salvation in Jewish circles in Paul's day, and there is some evidence of disagreement on this matter. Josephus tells the fascinating story of King Izates of Adiabene (AD 1–55), who was convinced by a certain Jew by the name of Ananias about the truth of the Jewish religion (*Ant.* 20:34–42 [20.2.3–20.2.4]). Still, Izates's mother Helena, who was a convert to Judaism herself, worried about the political consequences of Izates receiving circumcision and being identified as Jewish. Ananias assured Izates that circumcision wasn't necessary to worship God and that he could be forgiven for not adhering strictly to the law. Ananias advocated a laxer approach to the law, yet he did not do so for principled reasons but because of pragmatic concerns. He wanted to spare Izates from negative political consequences that could come from being circumcised. Nevertheless, another Jew, Eleazar, came along and admonished Izates to be circumcised (*Ant.* 20:43–46 [20.2.4]), emphasizing that the law plainly required it. Izates was convinced and was circumcised. We have seen from the

---

5   Jubilees may have reached its final composition around 100 BC.

Old Testament texts discussed above why Eleazar's case was more convincing than Ananias's. It seems quite obvious that the Old Testament demands that converts to the Jewish faith must be circumcised.

Even though some Jews (like Ananias) downplayed the requirement to be circumcised for one to be converted to Judaism, it seems that the necessity of circumcision for conversion was the majority position in Israel, and the story of Ananias, Izates, and Eleazar confirms such a perspective.[6] As noted above, a natural reading of the torah is that physical circumcision was necessary to be in covenant with God. Of course, spiritual circumcision was also emphasized in Jewish circles, but this was not new in the Second Temple period since the demand for circumcision of the heart goes back to the Old Testament as well (Deut. 10:16; 30:6; Jer. 4:4). It is well known that Philo emphasized spiritual circumcision (*Spec. Laws* 1:6, 305), and that is hardly surprising given his well-known allegorical method. The spiritual was always more important than the physical for Philo as a Hellenizing Jew. Still, in a fascinating discussion Philo emphasizes that one must observe *both the spiritual and physical* dimensions of commands, applying this to both the Sabbath and circumcision (*Migr.* 89–93). Both physical and spiritual circumcision must be observed. Even a Jew such as Philo who prized the spiritual significance of circumcision still required physical circumcision. Thus, Paul's insistence on spiritual circumcision while dispensing with the need for physical circumcision was highly controversial (Rom. 2:28–29; Phil. 3:2–3; Col. 2:11–12) and fiercely opposed by some. We can see more clearly, then, why Paul's adversaries in Galatia criticized him. He was denying the covenant sign required in the law and in effect was denying the election of Israel as God's people.

The troublemakers subscribed not only to circumcision but also to the law of Moses as a whole. Those who accept circumcision for

---

6 For the minority view that circumcision wasn't required, see Neil McEleney, "Conversion, Circumcision, and the Law," *NTS* 20 (1974): 319–41. Supporting the view that circumcision was required for conversion, see John Nolland, "Uncircumcised Proselytes?," *JSJ* 12 (1981): 173–94; Shaye J. D. Cohen, "Crossing the Boundary and Becoming a Jew," *HTR* 82 (1989): 26–30.

salvation are also obligated to keep the entire law. I mentioned earlier the Pharisaic believers in Acts (15:1, 5) who demanded the observance of circumcision and the law of Moses. Putting circumcision and the law together was the standard Jewish view since circumcision is part of the law (cf. Lev. 12:3). There is every reason to believe, then, that the adversaries also promoted observance of the entirety of the law given to Moses, and the evidence in Galatians supports this connection. For instance, Paul links circumcision with the law when he charges the opponents with demanding circumcision, and yet they are not observers of the law themselves (Gal. 6:13). We have further evidence that the adversaries demanded observance of the entire law since the Galatians are addressed as those who "desire to be under the law" (4:21). Indeed, Paul connects submission to circumcision with observance of the entire law (5:3), showing again that the two are linked. Requiring circumcision means that one was attempting to be justified by the law (5:4). Observance of days, months, seasons, and years is mentioned (4:10), and given the emphasis on the law in the remainder of the letter we have good reasons to think that observances from the Old Testament law are in view. It seems, then, that the antagonists declared that one must be circumcised and keep the law to be right with God—to belong to the people of God. Paul's wide-ranging reflections on the law in Galatians (see Gal. 2:16, 19, 21; 3:2, 5, 10–12, 17, 19, 21, 23; 4:4; 5:14, 23) also support the idea that circumcision and law were inextricably intertwined. Thus, Paul had to set forth a theology of law in order to respond to the opponents.

Conclusion

The opponents in Galatia questioned Paul's apostolic legitimacy, claiming that his gospel was *dependent* on the Jerusalem apostles and that he *distorted* the gospel the twelve taught. Furthermore, they complained that Paul departed from the clear requirement that one must be circumcised to belong to the people of God. In doing so he was breaking the covenant that the Lord had established with his people. The Galatians, according to the adversaries, must submit to circumcision and observe the torah handed down from Moses to belong to the people of God. Such a perspective, they likely claimed, represented the historic position of the people of God for centuries. It was this perspective that Paul countered in the letter to the Galatians, and the rest of this book will sketch in the main elements of Paul's response.

2

Paul's Apostolic Authority

Introduction

The objections of the opponents to the Pauline gospel set the table for the remainder of this book. In this chapter we explore how Paul responded to questions about his apostolic legitimacy. In subsequent chapters Paul's theological response to the adversaries will be traced, and we shall see that Paul's gospel is fundamentally eschatological and apocalyptic. Those who demand circumcision have exalted circumcision over the cross of Christ, but the latter spells the irrelevance of the former. Indeed, the adversaries' insistence on circumcision amounts to justification by law instead of justification by faith. The law, then, must be understood in light of the Christ event and can't be transferred over into the new era as if Jesus Christ hasn't come. In the new era the family of Abraham, the people of God, has been redrawn, and daily life isn't oriented around the law but around the power of the Holy Spirit.

This survey of what is to come brings us back to the current chapter where the issue of Paul's apostolic authority will be examined. We saw in chapter 1 that the antagonists questioned Paul's apostolic legitimacy, claiming that he was dependent on the Jerusalem apostles and that he distorted the gospel taught by the twelve. Those claims provide the structure for this chapter. We shall see from Galatians 1–2 that Paul defended the notions that his gospel was *independent* from the twelve and that he *didn't distort* the gospel they taught. The order of the discussion is crucial because if Paul began by saying that he didn't veer away from what the twelve preached, that would feed into the narrative that he relied on the apostles for his gospel. Thus, he argues *first* that his gospel was independent, and only after he establishes his independence does he turn to the question of his relationship to the apostles in Jerusalem.

An Independent Gospel

The independence of the Pauline gospel comes to the forefront in Galatians 1, but we should notice that Paul's independence isn't a matter of personal autonomy or individual freedom, as if Paul were a person influenced by the Enlightenment and by the conception of freedom and liberty championed by Western culture. Paul's independence is set in the context of the truth of the gospel. He defends himself, but he isn't declaring his liberty because he prizes human autonomy and liberty. Paul's self-defense stems from his deeply held conviction that the message of the agitators was a radically different gospel, one that violated the truth of the gospel given to him by Jesus Christ. Paul was faced with a strange situation where he had to defend himself to uphold the truth of the gospel since his ministry and the message of the gospel were intertwined.

It is well-known that most Pauline letters have a thanksgiving after the initial greeting, but there is no thanksgiving in Galatians. Instead, he rebukes the readers (Gal. 1:6–9) since they were abandoning Christ's grace and were embracing an alien gospel, which was no gospel at all. Before Paul defends himself he reminds the readers what is at stake, and the matter before them is the truth of the gospel itself. By listening to the antagonists the Galatians were in peril of embracing a different gospel. Paul asserts in uncompromising terms that accepting any other gospel will bring a curse (*anathema*). Ultimately, the issue was not about Paul because if he changed course and began to proclaim a gospel that differed from what he preached at their conversion, he would be accursed as well (1:8). The issues facing the Galatians were not merely a matter of differing opinions. Paul reaffirms that an eschatological curse belongs to anyone who disseminates a gospel that clashes with the one the Galatians first embraced (1:9). This latter declaration almost certainly was directed against the opponents, against those who were proclaiming a gospel at variance with Paul's.

Apparently, the outside teachers charged Paul with adjusting his gospel, particularly on the matter of circumcision, to please people (Gal. 1:10; 5:11). Perhaps they pointed to instances where Paul circumcised others and claimed that he didn't say the same to the Galatians to mollify them, worried that it would upset them and perhaps lead them to reject his message. Paul countered that such a reading of his methods and motives was completely off target, for his insistence that the message of the gospel cannot and must not be negotiated verifies that his aim wasn't to please people. Still, as important as the motives and aims of Paul were, they were not the fundamental issue. The question was whether Paul's gospel was from God or whether it was derived from people. The adversaries charged that Paul's gospel hailed from the Jerusalem apostles, that he was dependent on their teaching. Paul averred that his gospel did not originate with human beings (1:11), that his gospel accords with the truth because it stemmed from God himself. The remainder of Galatians 1 develops, augments, and explains the claim that the Pauline gospel was not a human innovation but was a revelation from God in Christ.

Paul explicitly asserts that he didn't receive the gospel from anyone (he wasn't dependent!), nor did anyone teach him its contents (Gal. 1:12). Instead, the gospel was given to him "through a revelation of Jesus Christ" (1:12). This revelation took place on the Damascus road where Jesus Christ appeared to Paul and commissioned him as an apostle. This amazing story is recounted in thrilling detail three times in Acts (Acts 9, 22, 26). Since Paul saw Jesus Christ on the way to Damascus and since he was appointed by him to the apostolic office (1 Cor. 9:1–2), Paul didn't suffer from doubts about the truth of his gospel. Clearly he wasn't dependent on the twelve in Jerusalem for his gospel since he received it independently on the day he met Jesus Christ on the Damascus road.

Galatians 1:13–14 provides further evidence for the independence of the Pauline gospel. Paul rehearses in these verses his "former life in Judaism" (Gal. 1:13). Incidentally, the meaning of the word "Judaism" (*Ioudaismos*) is quite controversial, but it is probably adequate here to define it as a Jewish way of life based on the torah, with the understanding that various interpretations of the law circulated in Paul's day (see 2 Macc. 2:21; 8:1; 14:38; 4 Macc. 4:26).[1] Paul's adherence to the law before meeting Christ is verified in Acts where he says that he was "educated at the feet of Gamaliel according to the strict manner of the law of our fathers" (Acts 22:3). Before Herod Agrippa II (who lived to around AD 100) and the Procurator Festus (who ruled Judea AD 59–62), Paul declared that "according to the strictest party of our religion I have lived as a Pharisee" (Acts 26:5). We find the same perspective in Paul's own writing; he was "circumcised on the eighth day, of the people of Israel, of the tribe of Benjamin, a Hebrew of Hebrews; as to the law, a Pharisee" (Phil. 3:5). Paul was not neutral or passive about the torah before meeting Jesus Christ. He devoted himself ardently to the law, believing that obedience to it was the path of blessing. Before he met Jesus Christ, Paul would have agreed with the sentiments of the Mishnah: "Great is the Law, for it gives life to them that practice it both in this world and the world to come" (m. 'Abot 6:7).[2] The law was seen as the way of life, and again Paul would have agreed with the claim "the more study of the Law the more life" (m. 'Abot 2:7; cf. Sir. 45:5; 4 Ezra 14:30). Paul's radical change relative to the law, then, is nothing less than astonishing. I will postpone for the moment answering *why* Paul reminds the Galatians of his previous life, although it should be noted that this is the most important question in these verses. Still, before coming to the crucial *why* question, we should attend to the content of Galatians 1:13–14 as the pre-Christian life of Paul is described.[3]

1 Cf. Roy E. Ciampa, *The Presence and Function of Scripture in Galatians 1 and 2*, WUNT 2/102 (Tübingen: Mohr Siebeck, 1998), 107.
2 For Mishnaic citations, see *The Mishnah*, ed. Herbert Danby (London: Oxford University Press, 1933).
3 Some scholars maintain that Paul was not converted on the Damascus road but called to be an apostle. So Krister Stendahl, *Paul among Jews and Gentiles and Other Essays*

Before the Damascus road experience, Paul "persecuted" and "tried to destroy" God's church (Gal. 1:13). The book of Acts confirms Paul's persecuting activity (Acts 9:1–2, 4, 13–14; 22:4–5, 7–8, 19–20; 26:9–11), and Paul also describes himself as "a persecutor of the church" (Phil. 3:6). In 1 Timothy he describes himself as "a blasphemer, persecutor, and insolent opponent" of God's people (1 Tim. 1:13). Indeed, Paul believed he was "unworthy to be called an apostle, because I persecuted the church of God" (1 Cor. 15:9). A mistake should be avoided here, for some might think that Paul was consciously sinning in persecuting and opposing the church. But the situation was precisely the opposite. Paul's persecution of the church stemmed from his zeal for God and for the torah (Gal. 1:14; cf. Acts 22:3). Indeed, Philippians 3:6 specifically tells us that Paul persecuted the church because of his zeal, and this accords with Romans 10:2 where some have "a zeal for God" that is "not according to knowledge." Paul probably imagined himself as a new Phinehas since the latter, because of his intense zeal, put to death the Israelite man and Midianite woman who were having sex in sight of the tabernacle (Num. 25:6–13). Similarly, Paul likely saw himself as a new Elijah who in his zeal for the Lord put to death the prophets of Baal (1 Kings 18:40; 19:10, 14). Or even nearer to Paul's day was the example of the Hasmonean priest Mattathias who, when he saw an illegitimate sacrifice being offered in Israel under pagan influence, "burned with zeal," killing both the Jew offering the sacrifice and the soldier compelling him to do so (1 Macc. 2:24–26 NRSV; see also 1 Macc. 2:50, 54, 58). If this reading of Paul's aims is correct, we are given an important window into his thought. He persecuted the church because of his zeal for the torah and believed he was pleasing the Lord in doing so. He thought he was a modern-day Phinehas, Elijah, and Mattathias, standing up for the truth of God's word. He wasn't consciously

---

(Philadelphia: Fortress, 1977), 1–23; J. D. G. Dunn, *The Epistle to the Galatians*, BNTC (Peabody, MA: Hendrickson, 1993), 65. It is more convincing, however, to argue that Paul was both called and converted so that the two are not pitted against one another. See Peter O'Brien, "Was Paul Converted?," in *The Paradoxes of Paul*, vol. 2 of *Justification and Variegated Nomism*, ed. D. A. Carson, Peter T. O'Brien, and Mark A. Seifrid (Grand Rapids, MI: Baker, 2004), 361–91.

rebelling against the Lord but thought that he was honoring him with his devotion. Paul's life fits with Jesus's words, "They will put you out of the synagogues. Indeed, the hour is coming when whoever kills you will think he is offering service to God" (John 16:2). Paul was convinced that he was serving God in his zeal.

Paul goes on to say that his zeal for the traditions handed down by his ancestors was such that he was known and celebrated for his commitment to the Lord (Gal. 1:14). He was, if we think in today's terms, the incredibly bright seminary student or the gifted young scholar from whom people expected great things in the future.

Why does Paul rehearse the story of his life in Judaism in Galatians 1:13–14? Paul's history supports the claim that he received his gospel as a supernatural revelation from Jesus Christ. He had no earthly reason to transfer his allegiance to Jesus Christ. He certainly did not confess Jesus as the Messiah to please people. If Paul's desire were to garner commendation from others, he would have remained within the circle of Judaism since he was lauded and praised as the young student who was intellectually gifted and ardently committed to the faith. He didn't become a slave of Christ because his life in Judaism was miserable. Quite the contrary. As a young rabbinic student he was receiving plaudits from others, and the same didn't happen when he gave himself to Jesus Christ. There was no earthly reason, then, for him to leave Judaism and confess Jesus as Messiah. After all, he only was persecuted after he devoted himself to Jesus, not before. The best explanation for his turnaround was that Jesus Christ appeared to him on the Damascus road. Thus, the claim that Paul was pleasing people in not requiring circumcision was ridiculous, for the story of Paul's call demonstrates that his motive was not to please people.

Galatians 1:15–17 confirms that Paul's gospel was revealed to him by Jesus himself. What explains Paul's radical change so that the former persecutor became a fervent evangelist of Jesus Christ? Paul doesn't take any credit for his change of mind; he does not appeal to his own wisdom, insight, perceptiveness, or new insight from the Scriptures. Instead, he gives God the praise for his transformation. As Paul reflects on how Jesus revealed himself to him on the Damascus road, he appropriates the calling of the prophets in the Old Testament to explain how the Lord called and converted him. Paul's calling evokes the callings of Jeremiah and Isaiah as prophets.[4] The Lord declared to Jeremiah,

> Before I formed you in the womb I knew you,
> and before you were born I consecrated you;
> I appointed you a prophet to the nations. (Jer. 1:5)

Isaiah reflects on his prophetic calling in similar terms:

> The LORD called me from the womb,
> from the body of my mother he named my name. (Isa. 49:1)

So too, Paul was set apart before his birth and was effectually called by God's grace (Gal. 1:15).[5] Paul could not take any credit for his apostolic calling since his vocation was due entirely to the compelling and constraining grace of God. God revealed his Son, Jesus Christ, to Paul on his way to Damascus, and thus Paul didn't need to consult others or seek out apostolic approval of his gospel before he began to preach (Gal. 1:16–17). Paul received the gospel independently of any human agent, and thus the gospel he proclaimed was from Jesus Christ himself and could not be ascribed to any human being.

The independence of Paul's gospel explains the last six verses of the chapter (Gal. 1:18–24), as Paul emphasizes his independence from the apostles. He didn't visit with Peter for three years, and even then the only other apostle he saw was James, the Lord's brother. Paul interrupts the discussion by insisting that his words are truthful and that he isn't lying (Gal. 1:20). Such words would be completely unnecessary if Paul

---

4 See Karl O. Sandnes, *Paul—One of the Prophets? A Contribution to the Apostle's Self-Understanding*, WUNT 2/43 (Tübingen: J. C. B. Mohr, 1991).
5 For the notion that Paul was taking on the vocation of the servant of the Lord (cf. Gal 2:20; Acts 13:47), see Matthew S. Harmon, "She Must and Shall Go Free: Paul's Isaianic Gospel in Galatians" (PhD diss., Wheaton College Graduate School, 2006), 104–7, 138–60.

weren't under attack as an apostle, and they demonstrate that Paul's veracity and apostleship were being questioned. Finally, Paul stresses that the churches in Judea didn't know him either (Gal. 1:21–24), reaffirming again his independence.

A Ratified Gospel

Paul establishes the independence of his gospel in Galatians 1, but we need to remember that there were two charges against Paul. The antagonists claimed that he both *depended* on the twelve apostles and that he *distorted* their gospel. In Galatians 2 Paul responds to the accusation that he distorted their gospel and claims that the allegation is radically mistaken. The apostolic pillars didn't disagree with the Pauline gospel but ratified, endorsed, and verified it when they heard it.

Paul explains in Galatians 2 that he went up to Jerusalem in accord with a revelation (undoubtedly direction from the Spirit that he should make this visit) fourteen years later, which was probably fourteen years after his conversion (Gal. 2:1–2). He didn't travel to Jerusalem to receive apostolic approbation but to present the gospel to Peter, James, and John. The fact that he went fourteen years after his conversion demonstrates that he didn't travel to Jerusalem to solicit approval for his gospel. But then Paul seems to contradict such a reading when he explains that he went to Jerusalem "to make sure I was not running or had not run in vain" (2:2). What Paul says could be read to say that he had doubts about his gospel, that he needed the confirmation of the apostles to certify that he was really on target. But this interpretation should be rejected because it contradicts everything Paul says in Galatians 1. He had no doubts about his gospel, for he had received it directly through an appearance of Jesus to him on the Damascus road. Nothing could ever make him doubt what he saw on that life-changing day. Thus, we have to probe deeper to discern the meaning of Paul's statement. Paul wasn't plagued with doubts about his gospel, but he was a realist, and he knew that, practically speaking, his efforts in spreading the gospel would be thwarted if the Jerusalem apostles disagreed with him.⁶ Paul was entirely convinced that his gospel was true, and he didn't harbor any doubts about its truthfulness, but pragmatically his evangelistic efforts would be frustrated if supporters of the apostles informed the churches where Paul ministered that the apostles in Jerusalem disagreed with him. Thus, Paul needed apostolic agreement to advance his apostolic mission and message. Otherwise, adversaries would dog him in church after church and point out that the pillar apostles in Jerusalem had a different view.

Paul proceeds to relay to the Galatians the story of what happened in the case of Titus (Gal. 2:3–5). The rendition of the story is exceedingly brief, and we would love to hear more details, but Paul gives us instead only the results of the meeting. We need to recognize that the account represents what happened *in Jerusalem* some time before the controversy erupted among the Galatian Christians. Paul isn't talking about what happened in Galatia. Since Titus was a Gentile, some in Jerusalem insisted that he had to be circumcised in order to be saved in accord with the torah, and Paul identifies these infiltrators as "false brothers" (2:4). Perhaps the Jerusalem apostles wavered to some extent and perhaps they even thought it was a good idea for Titus to be circumcised, though what the Jerusalem apostles thought and did at the outset is speculation. At the end of the day, Peter, James, and John did not compel (*anankazō*, 2:3) Titus to be circumcised. They agreed with Paul and Barnabas that circumcision wasn't required for salvation. In the midst of the debate, Paul didn't vacillate for a second, resisting the imposition of circumcision "so that the truth of the gospel might be preserved for you" (2:5). What stands out in this story is that the apostles in Jerusalem confirmed the Pauline gospel, and thus they did not require Titus to be circumcised.

Incidentally, we must not confuse what was decided in Titus's case with Paul's agreement to circumcise Timothy in Acts 16. The two cases were completely different. Timothy was considered to be a Jew because he was the son of a Jewish mother, even though his father was a Gentile (Acts

---

6 So also J. Louis Martyn, *Galatians*, AB (New Haven, CT: Yale University Press, 1997), 193.

16:1, 3). Titus was not half Jewish but was a Gentile, which is what Paul means in identifying him as a "Greek" (Gal. 2:3). In Timothy's case, Paul circumcised him since he was considered to be Jewish, applying the knife to Timothy so that he could bring him into the Jewish synagogues and do evangelism. Nor should we miss the fact that he only circumcised Timothy *after* Acts 15, where it was decided that circumcision wasn't necessary for salvation. He didn't circumcise Timothy for his salvation but to facilitate mission among the Jews. Titus, as a Gentile, was a remarkably different case. Paul wouldn't hear even for a second the demand to circumcise Titus since that would imply one had to observe the law and be circumcised to be saved. By refusing to circumcise Titus, Paul upheld the truth of the gospel.

The ratification of Paul's gospel by the pillar apostles (Peter, James, and John) is impressed on readers more fully in Galatians 2:6–10. Paul boldly and confidently declares that the apostles in Jerusalem added nothing to his gospel (2:6). Paul may sound boastful, but his point is that the gospel, not the stature of any human being (not even an apostle), is the final authority. The Galatians had to beware of venerating the twelve, for they were merely human beings after all, and praise and complete trust should be reserved for God alone.[7] Paul, however, proceeds to the main point in Galatians 2:7–9. James, Peter, and John recognized that Paul was "entrusted" by God with the message of the gospel and that his ministry was just as valid as Peter's (2:7). James, Peter, and John are identified as "pillars" (2:9), probably because they are conceived of as playing a key role in God's temple—the church.[8] This fits with Paul's claim in Ephesians that the church is "built on the foundation of the apostles and prophets" (Eph. 2:20). As the pillars of the church, they extended a hand in partnership to Paul and Barnabas, recognizing their ministry to the Gentiles. In other words, Paul and Barnabas were *equal partners* in the gospel and not subordinate to the twelve.

---

7   Paul refers here to the status of James, Peter, and John as apostles. See Simon Gathercole, "The Petrine and Pauline *Sola Fide* in Galatians 2," in *Lutherische und Neue Paulusperspektive: Beiträge zu einem Schlüsselproblem der gegenwärtigen exegetischen Diskussion*, ed. Michael Bachmann, WUNT 182 (Tübingen: Mohr Siebeck, 2005), 317.

8   Ulrich Wilckens, "στῦλος," *TDNT* 7:735; Martyn, *Galatians*, 205.

We see, then, that Paul dismantles the second major criticism of the antagonists. The antagonists asserted that Paul distorted the apostolic gospel, but the pillars didn't agree. Quite the contrary. They recognized God's grace in Paul's ministry and realized that the gospel Paul taught was the true gospel, the same gospel they proclaimed.[9] We find something similar in 1 Corinthians 15:1–11 where Paul rehearses the gospel, focusing on Jesus's death for the forgiveness of sins and his resurrection. A series of people who saw the resurrected Lord are then recorded, but Paul closes (1 Cor. 15:11) by noting that the same gospel was preached and believed by all those who have seen the risen Lord. Included in Paul's purview here in 1 Corinthians are the twelve (1 Cor. 15:5) and the apostles (1 Cor. 15:7). The opponents in Galatia, then, were wrong on both counts. Paul's gospel wasn't dependent on Jerusalem but independent, and yet he didn't distort the gospel preached by the pillars but faithfully proclaimed the same gospel as they did.

The last step of Paul's defense is found in Galatians 2:11–21, and it isn't my purpose to unfold the fullness of this text. Here we find the famous incident in Antioch where Peter and other Jews were eating together with Gentiles. Apparently, James in Jerusalem heard about what was happening and sent a message to Peter, warning him about the consequences of eating with Gentiles. We don't know precisely what James said, but it was enough to persuade Peter so that he dissociated from eating with the Gentiles. Paul informs us that Peter was motivated by fear (presumably of persecution) instead of by conviction.[10] Peter, of course, had enormous influence so that the rest of the Jews followed his example, and what must have been particularly difficult for Paul was that Barnabas—his partner on the first missionary journey (Acts 13–14)—sided with Peter. Paul responded by rebuking Peter for his volte-face, reminding him that he had departed from "the truth of the gospel" (Gal. 2:14).

9 See Han Dieter Betz, *Galatians: A Commentary on Paul's Letter to the Churches in Galatia*, Hermeneia (Philadelphia: Fortress, 1979), 100; Richard N. Longenecker, *Galatians*, WBC (Dallas: Word, 1990), 58; Frank J. Matera, *Galatians*, SP (Collegeville, MN: Liturgical Press, 1992), 77.

10 See the discussion in D. A. Carson, *Love in Hard Places* (Wheaton, IL: Crossway, 2002), 150–60.

Paul recounts this story to underscore that his gospel was true and that it was recognized as such even by the apostle Peter.[11] He doesn't tell the story to humiliate or embarrass Peter, nor is it warranted to deduce from this account that Peter and Paul remained enemies for the rest of their lives (as many historical-critical scholars assert). Peter's response to Paul isn't recorded, but the aim of the story wasn't to chronicle the relationship between Peter and Paul. Actually, I think there are good reasons to think that Peter responded to Paul's reproof. If Peter actually ended up disagreeing with Paul permanently, the claim that Peter, James, and John recognized the truth of his gospel in Galatians 2:1–10 would have been meaningless. The opponents would rightly object over against Paul that once Peter understood the practical implications of Paul's gospel he disagreed with it. If this were the case, then, Paul's claim of apostolic support in 2:1–10 would have been disingenuous. Paul's argument only works on the supposition that Peter finally agreed with him, and Paul could hardly paper over this matter if Peter resisted his reproof.

Supporting a positive response from Peter is the verb used to describe the impact of Peter's actions on the Gentiles. Peter's refusal to eat with the Gentiles had the effect of *compelling* (*anankazō*) Gentiles to live like Jews (Gal. 2:14). The verb *anankazō* is the same one used to describe the "false brothers" who attempted to force Titus to be circumcised (Gal. 2:3–5). As the subsequent verses demonstrate (Gal. 2:15–21), if Peter continued to insist that the Gentiles eat kosher, he would be promoting a false gospel and would be in the same situation as the false brothers. Still, Peter differed from the false brothers in a very important respect since he acted *hypocritically* and not out of conviction.[12] We also see in a later letter that Peter preached the same gospel as Paul (1 Cor. 15:1–11),

---

11 Peter Richardson, "Pauline Inconsistency: I Corinthians 9.19–23 and Galatians 2.11–14," *NTS* 26 (1979–80): 347–62, claims Paul was in the wrong and that Peter followed Paul's principle of contextualization in 1 Cor. 9:19–23. For a convincing rebuttal, see D. A. Carson, "Pauline Inconsistency: Reflections on I Corinthians 9.19–23 and Galatians 2.11–14," *Churchman* 100 (1986): 6–45.

12 On hypocrisy, see Ciampa, *The Presence of Scripture in Galatians 1 and 2*, 167–68, who references 2 Macc. 6:24–26 and 4 Macc. 6:17.

and thus Peter must have responded positively to Paul's correction.[13] Prior to this he was inadvertently supporting the perspective of the false brothers. This brings us back to the main purpose of the paragraph. Paul's reproof of Peter shows that his gospel was authoritative and from Jesus Christ. In this chapter Paul informs the Galatians that Peter, James, and John recognized and validated Paul's gospel (Gal. 2:1–10). But his argument is even stronger. The Pauline gospel, received from Jesus Christ on the Damascus road, was authoritative over Peter when he strayed (Gal. 2:11–14). The Jerusalem apostles both recognized and submitted to the Pauline gospel. Paul had not distorted the apostolic gospel. Quite the contrary. The pillar apostles taught the same gospel.

Conclusion

We have seen in this chapter that the antagonists disputed the Pauline gospel on the grounds that it was *dependent* on Jerusalem and a *distortion* of the apostolic message. Paul responds to these charges by reminding the Galatians that he received the gospel *independently* when Jesus Christ appeared to him and commissioned him on the road to Damascus. The dramatic change in Paul's life from a Jewish way of life to being a follower of Christ occurred because Christ revealed himself to Paul. As a consequence Paul didn't consult with the apostles or any others to substantiate his gospel since he received it from Christ himself. At the same time, when the Jerusalem apostles actually heard the Pauline gospel, they did not dissent from it but *verified its truth*. Indeed, the Pauline gospel even called Peter to repentance when he strayed. Thus, both charges against Paul were false. He wasn't dependent on the twelve, and yet at the same time his gospel wasn't a distortion of what the apostles taught. The latter recognized that Paul proclaimed the same gospel that they preached. Paul has defended the legitimacy of his apostleship in Galatians 1–2, and thus in the rest of the letter he is now prepared to defend the content of the gospel he proclaimed.

---

13 Rightly Eckhard J. Schnabel, *Early Christian Mission*, 2 vols. (Downers Grove, IL: InterVarsity Press, 2004), 2:1005-6.

PART 2

———

THE GOSPEL

3

Eschatology and Apocalyptic

Introduction

As stated above, the remainder of the book explores different dimensions of the Pauline gospel in Galatians. In this chapter the framework that permeates Paul's understanding in the letter is sketched in. Virtually all scholars recognize the eschatological character of Paul's theology, and Galatians is no exception. It should be said, however, that in recent years a kind of war has been going on in Pauline studies. Is his gospel eschatological or apocalyptic? Or another way we could put it is this: Was his gospel salvation-historical or apocalyptic? The eschatological / salvation-historical reading sees Paul's gospel as fulfilling Old Testament prophecy, standing in a historical line of continuity with Old Testament revelation and realizing the covenant promises made in the Old Testament.[1] The apocalyptic reading, on the other hand, stresses the sudden irruption into history of God's saving act in Christ Jesus.[2] God's salvation in Christ

---

[1] For proponents of this view, see e.g., Herman N. Ridderbos, *Paul: An Outline of His Theology*, trans. J. R. de Witt (Grand Rapids, MI: Eerdmans, 1975); N. T. Wright, *Paul and the Faithfulness of God*, vol. 4 of *Christian Origins and the Question of God* (Minneapolis: Fortress, 2013); G. K. Beale, *A New Testament Biblical Theology: The Unfolding of the Old Testament in the New* (Grand Rapids, MI: Baker Academic, 2011); Richard B. Gaffin Jr., *In the Fullness of Time: An Introduction to the Biblical Theology of Acts and Paul* (Wheaton, IL: Crossway, 2022).

[2] For the apocalyptic reading, see J. Louis Martyn, "Apocalyptic Antinomies in Paul's Letter to the Galatians," *NTS* 31 (1985): 410–24; J. C. Beker, *The Triumph of God: The Essence*

doesn't represent a neat, linear fulfillment of what happened previously but a dramatic and sudden intervention into history.

This book isn't a technical study that dives into the details of this dispute in Pauline studies. But I suggest that the war between these two schools is a false polarity since Paul's theology is both eschatological and apocalyptic. The gospel fulfills Old Testament promises, and the story beginning in the Old Testament reaches its consummation in Jesus Christ. But at the same time, the promises are fulfilled in a stunning and invasive act of God in Jesus Christ. We don't have a neat, clean, and linear story of the fulfillment of God's promises. No one could claim such even in the Old Testament! God's purposes advance and then seem to retreat—Israel obeys and then rebels. God's purposes aren't fulfilled in a beautiful arc that curves upward in a smooth and unbroken narrative. Instead, the story of God's salvation is full of fits and starts, with advances and retreats. In fact, by the time the New Testament opens it seems that the hope for redemption had ground to a halt forever, but suddenly God acts and invades the present world in Jesus Christ. The end-time promises were fulfilled but in a startling and shocking way—both eschatologically and apocalyptically! I realize that in such a short space I haven't demonstrated that the fulfillment is both eschatological and apocalyptic. I have asserted it more than proved it, but it will be a presupposition in the ensuing discussion.

New Creation

Paul only uses the expression "new creation" once in the letter (Gal. 6:15), but the notion isn't restricted to the phrase. Indeed, the new creation surfaces in the first verse, which affirms that God raised Jesus from the dead (Gal. 1:1). The resurrection in Jewish thought means that the new age has arrived and that the old age of evil and death has

---

of Paul's Thought (Minneapolis: Fortress, 1990); Douglas A. Campbell, *The Deliverance of God: An Apocalyptic Rereading of Justification in Paul* (Grand Rapids, MI: Eerdmans, 2009); Martinus de Boer, *Galatians*, NTL (Louisville: Westminster John Knox, 2011). It should be noted that Beker thinks Galatians isn't apocalyptic, but Martyn and others dispute that claim. For a survey of the movement along with analysis, see Jamie Davis, *The Apocalyptic Paul: Retrospect and Prospect* (Eugene, OR: Cascade, 2022).

come to an end.[3] Isaiah prophesies that the Lord "will swallow up death forever" and tears will be a distant memory (Isa. 25:8). Similarly, those who are raised from the dead will experience "everlasting life" and will shine "like the stars forever and ever" (Dan. 12:2–3; see also Isa. 26:19). On the day of the resurrection the Lord's promises to his people will be fulfilled, and the people of God will be restored and unified (Ezek. 37:1–14). The resurrection of Jesus means that the old age has ended, and thus Paul foreshadows the argument of the entire letter. Circumcision is no longer required because it was a permanent ordinance in the old era while the old creation persisted. Now that the new creation has come, the ordinances of the old age have passed away. Commands like circumcision only apply under the old covenant and in the old era, but the resurrection represents the apocalyptic irruption of the new age, and thus the regulations of the former age have expired.

Paul has died and now he lives to God (Gal. 2:19). In other words, he has "been crucified with Christ," and now Christ "lives in" him (2:20). Paul speaks representatively so that what is true of him applies to all believers in Jesus everywhere. They have died and come to life again. This is another way of describing an apocalyptic inbreaking through Christ Jesus. The new creation has come, and this is evident since Paul and all believers have died and come to life again. The power of the resurrection has, like a sneaker wave, washed up into the old age and taken over the shoreline of the beach. Now believers live in the new creation inaugurated by Christ's resurrection. The new age has broken in and the old age is set aside. The arrival of the new creation in Christ's resurrection affects every theme in Galatians, whether it is justification, the law, the people of God, or life in the Spirit. Still, a fuller explication of these themes will be worked out in subsequent chapters.

The eschatological and apocalyptic dimensions of Paul's gospel are apparent in Galatians 1:4 where Christ "gave himself for our sins to deliver us from the present evil age." The term "deliver" (*exaireō*) presents Jesus's death as an exodus type of rescue (see Ex. 3:8; 18:4, 8, 9, 10 LXX).

---

3 See the outstanding work by N. T. Wright, *The Resurrection of the Son of God*, vol. 3 of *Christian Origins and the Question of God* (Minneapolis: Fortress, 2003).

The same verb is used for the Lord's promise to liberate his people in a second exodus foretold in the prophets (Isa. 31:5; 60:16; Ezek. 34:27 LXX).[4] A distinction between this age and the age to come was common in Jewish thought (see 1 En. 71:15; 4 Ezra 4:27; 7:12–13, 50, 113–14; 8:1; 2 Bar. 14:13; 15:8; 44:8–15; CD 6.10–11, 14; 12.23; 1QpHab 5.7–8), and we find it fairly often in Jesus's teaching as well (Matt. 12:32; 13:39, 40, 49; 24:3; 28:20; Mark 10:30; Luke 18:30; 20:35). The contrast between the two ages also marks Paul's thought (Eph. 1:21). The present age is characterized by evil, and Satan exercises his dominion as the god of this present era (2 Cor. 4:4). Unbelievers are dazzled by the wisdom of this age (1 Cor. 1:20; 3:18), and the rulers of this age demonstrated their lack of perception by crucifying the Lord Jesus (1 Cor. 2:6, 8). Demas's love for the present world (2 Tim. 4:10) shows that he belongs to this world instead of the coming one (Eph. 2:2). Still, the new age, which is another way of talking about the new creation, has also invaded the present cosmos. "The end of the ages" has now come in Jesus Christ (1 Cor. 10:11). Jesus rules as Lord, as the reigning King during this age, and his rule will reach its climax in the age to come (Eph. 1:21; cf. 1 Cor. 15:24–28; Eph. 2:7). Since the new age has dawned through Christ's death and resurrection (Titus 2:12), believers have received the grace to live in a godly way, in a way that defies the rulers of the present era. On the other hand, life in the new age isn't easy since the age to come has been inaugurated but not consummated (1 Cor. 7:31). The battle with evil continues (Gal. 5:17), and thus believers must not be captured by riches (1 Tim. 6:17) and must resist being conformed to this present age (Rom. 12:2).

The "new creation," which closes the letter (Gal. 6:15), functions as an inclusio with the resurrection (1:1) and the coming of the new age (1:4), which open the letter. The Pauline statement about the new creation and its placement at the conclusion of the letter illustrate how important it is. The promise of the new creation reaches back to Isaiah 65:17 and 66:22

---

4 See Roy E. Ciampa, *The Presence and Function of Scripture in Galatians 1 and 2*, WUNT 2/102 (Tübingen: Mohr Siebeck, 1998), 61–62, n. 104; Todd A. Wilson, "Wilderness Apostasy and Paul's Portrayal of the Crisis in Galatians," *NTS* 50 (2004): 555–57.

where a new world is promised in which death is conquered, tears are a thing of the past, and wolves and lambs graze peacefully together.[5] The violence, hatred, bloodshed, and grief that stain the present world will come to an end. Since circumcision is particularly controverted in the Galatian churches, Paul declares here that both circumcision and uncircumcision are matters of indifference (Gal. 6:15; see also 5:6). The passion with which the opponents promoted circumcision demonstrated that they didn't know the time in which they were living; they were acting as if the time of fulfillment had not arrived. Remarkably, the same would be true if someone wanted to boast in uncircumcision, as if opposition to circumcision is what characterized Paul's ministry. Focusing on either circumcision or uncircumcision reveals a blindness to the apocalyptic act of God in Jesus Christ as the crucified and risen one. We understand, then, why in the previous verse (Gal. 6:14) Paul declares that he has been crucified to the world (the old order) and the world has been crucified to him. A death has taken place that radically changes the values, attachments, and loves that animate believers. The crucifixion of Paul and all believers to the world occurred when they were crucified with Christ (Gal. 2:20). A radical disruption has taken place so that the love for the present world has been severed at the cross. Old polarities, such as whether one is circumcised or uncircumcised, are fundamentally irrelevant. What matters is whether someone is part of the new creation that has dawned in Jesus Christ. Such a perspective accords with what Paul affirms in 2 Corinthians 5:17. The arrival of the new creation means that the old has passed away.

The new creation is also painted as the heavenly Jerusalem (Gal. 4:26). The heavenly Jerusalem is another world, a heavenly world, a transcendent world. We might think that the heavenly world has nothing to do with the here and now, but apparently the heavenly world intersects even now with the present creation because Paul says that the heavenly Jerusalem is the mother of believers. Those who belong to Christ are now members of this transcendent city, and thus they

---

5   For this reading of Isa. 65:17–25, see G. K. Beale, "An Amillennial Response to a Premillennial View of Isaiah 65:20," *JETS* 61 (2018): 461–92.

experience the freedom promised in the eschaton. Paul is not alone in speaking of the heavenly Jerusalem (cf. Heb. 12:22; Rev. 3:12; 21:2, 10; cf. 2 Bar. 4:2). The heavenly city to come has invaded the present evil age, and so we have an example of Paul's already-but-not-yet eschatology.[6] The Jerusalem above points to the new creation (Isa. 65:17; 66:1), for in Isaiah the new creation and the heavenly Jerusalem are closely linked (Isa. 65:18–19). In Isaiah 66:7–11, Zion gives birth to children, and their birth signifies the fulfillment of God's promises, which will lead to joy and gladness. The problem with the opponents is that they were living as if the new creation had not arrived, as if the old creation were still the predominant reality. They had made their home in the old Zion instead of the new Zion.

The Eschatological Spirit

The Spirit's work in transforming the lives of believers is the subject of chapter 8, but in this chapter I consider the Spirit as an eschatological/apocalyptic gift.[7] The apocalyptic work of the Spirit surfaces in the contrast between the Spirit and the flesh. The flesh represents the old person and what human beings are in Adam since through Adam sin and death came into the world (Rom. 5:12–14). The Spirit, on the other hand, will be given when God's apocalyptic and eschatological promises are realized, when the new era commences. The Galatians will revert back to the old era of salvation history if, "having begun by the Spirit," they then try to be "perfected by the flesh" (Gal. 3:3). The new era has begun, but since the new and old ages overlap, there is a threat that the Galatians will fall back into the old age (cf. Gal. 1:4). This is not a minor or inconsequential matter since the Spirit and flesh stand in radical opposition to each other (Gal. 5:16–18), just as the old age and new age cannot be reconciled. Believers are summoned to live by the

---

6 See Andrew T. Lincoln, *Paradise Now and Not Yet: Studies in the Role of the Heavenly Dimension in Paul's Thought with Special Reference to His Eschatology*, SNTSMS 43 (Cambridge: Cambridge University Press, 1981), 21–22.

7 See Jarvis W. Williams, *The Spirit, Ethics, and Eternal Life: Paul's Vision for the Christian Life* (Downers Grove, IL: IVP Academic, 2023); Gordon D. Fee, *God's Empowering Presence: The Holy Spirit in the Letters of Paul* (Peabody, MA: Hendrickson, 1994).

Spirit in accord with the new era that has dawned with Christ's death and resurrection (see also 5:22, 25; 6:8).

The antagonism between the flesh and the Spirit is also evident because those in the flesh persecute and oppose those who have the Spirit (Gal. 4:29). The attempt to impose the law by the Jewish teachers doesn't represent a legitimate alternative perspective or point of view. Their teaching has a fleshly origin, and their antagonism toward the Galatian believers demonstrates their resistance to the things of the Spirit. Believers, by way of contrast, know that the new era has arrived because they have received the Spirit by faith and because miracles are taking place in their midst (3:2, 5). The reception of the Spirit certifies the arrival of the new era since it represents a supernatural work of God and can't be attributed to the work, devotion, or piety of human beings. The latter may seem impressive, but at the end of the day it is nothing other than the work of the flesh (3:3).

The eschatological work of the Spirit is promised in a number of Old Testament texts. As he considers the desolation in Israel because of sin (Isa. 32:14), Isaiah links the gift of the Spirit with the new creation. A new day is coming when

> the Spirit is poured upon us from on high,
>   and the wilderness becomes a fruitful field,
>   and the fruitful field is deemed a forest.
> Then justice will dwell in the wilderness,
>   and righteousness abide in the fruitful field.
> And the effect of righteousness will be peace,
>   and the result of righteousness, quietness and trust forever.
> My people will abide in a peaceful habitation,
>   in secure dwellings, and in quiet resting places. (Isa. 32:15–18)

The new creation theme is quite evident in that the fields, forests, and the wilderness will be transformed when the Spirit is poured out. Furthermore, righteousness will become a reality and peace will settle over the land instead of conflict and war. Israel will experience rest and joy when the old age ceases and the new age dawns. Joel also promises the pouring out of the Spirit in the last day (Joel 2:28–32), and once again the result is a new creation, a transformed world. The Spirit is democratized and dispensed to all people without exception so that the gift of the Spirit isn't limited to religious leaders. As a result both men and women will prophesy, and

> your old men shall dream dreams,
> and your young men shall see visions. (Joel 2:28)

The crowning gift is eschatological salvation for all everywhere who call upon the Lord.

In Galatians 3:14 where the blessing of Abraham is equated with the promise of the Spirit, Paul alludes to Isaiah 44:3, which reads,

> For I will pour water on the thirsty land,
> and streams on the dry ground;
> I will pour my Spirit upon your offspring,
> and my blessing on your descendants.

The correspondence between the Spirit and the blessing in Galatians 3:14 is derived from Isaiah 44:3 where the Hebrew parallelism shows that the Spirit and blessing are two different ways of describing God's gifts for his people. The Spirit again seems to be connected with the new creation since a world that is desiccated and desolate will flourish with life when the Spirit is given. The result is that those who receive the Spirit are assured that they truly belong to the Lord and identify themselves as Israel (Isa. 44:5). Paul probably appropriates this verse in Galatians 6:16, where the church of Jesus Christ made up of both Jews and Gentiles is identified as the Israel of God—the restored Israel. The true Israel is characterized by those who have received the Spirit.

In Ezekiel 36 the gift of the Spirit signals the coming of the new creation as well. When the Lord grants his Spirit, Israel will return from exile in a new exodus (Ezek. 36:24), and we have already seen that the new exodus is also an apocalyptic reality. Also the Lord will cleanse his people from their sin and from idols so that they are no longer defiled and stained by evil (Ezek. 36:25). The "heart of stone" will be replaced with "a heart of flesh," and they will be granted "a new heart" and "a new spirit" (Ezek. 36:26). The Lord's work is radically new—we could say *apocalyptically* new—in that he will cause the Spirit to indwell his people (Ezek. 36:27), and as a consequence the people of God will keep the torah. The fulfillment of the law (Gal. 5:14)—the law of Christ (Gal. 6:2)—is another indication that the day of fulfillment has arrived.

Slavery and Freedom

All the themes we are investigating are closely related and intertwined to some extent with one another. Another dimension of the eschatological/apocalyptic character of Paul's gospel is the contrast between slavery and freedom. Israel received the law mediated by Moses on Mount Sinai (Gal. 3:20) so that they would live in a way that pleased God. The law described what it means to live under Yahweh's lordship and authority. Israel had been freed from Egyptian slavery, and the next question was whether they would live in true freedom or give way to evil. Unfortunately, the history of Israel was such that life under the law did not lead to the freedom they so desired. After possessing the land under Joshua it seemed that Israel was poised to enjoy the inheritance granted by Yahweh. The book of Judges, however, paints a startlingly different picture. Instead of Israel influencing the nations in the land of Canaan, Israel compromised with the cultures and gods of the land and often abandoned their covenant with the Lord. Israel forsook the Lord and served other gods. They flouted the stipulations of the covenant repeatedly, giving themselves to murder, adultery, lying, stealing, and so on.

After the reign of Solomon, the nation split into the southern (Judah) and northern kingdoms (Israel) under Rehoboam and Jeroboam. None of the northern kings in Israel worshiped and followed Yahweh according to the prescriptions of the Mosaic covenant. Some of the southern kings in Judah were faithful, but the south also slowly descended into sin. The prophets reminded both Israel and Judah of their covenant obligations, calling both kingdoms to repent. Still, both the north and the south refused to listen. The north was exiled by Assyria in 722 BC, and the south by Babylon in 586 BC. We could characterize life under the law, then, as one that led to slavery instead of freedom. We see in the history of Israel both subjugation to sin and captivity to foreign powers. The torah did not liberate Israel and Judah but pronounced judgment on them.

Israel's captivity didn't mean that Yahweh had abandoned his people. The prophets promised return from exile, and it became a reality in 536 BC in the new exodus. Still, the stunning promises found in the prophets were not realized fully. The prophets looked forward to a new exodus, a new covenant, a new David, and a new creation. What Israel experienced when it returned from Babylon, however, didn't match these promises. We find a fascinating example of this in the book of Ezra. Around 450 BC, Israel was back in the land; but Ezra characterizes their experience as "a little reviving in our slavery" (Ezra 9:8), and then he goes on to say, "We are slaves. Yet our God has not forsaken us in our slavery" (Ezra 9:9). The Israelites in the land of Israel were not literally slaves of the Persians, but they were under the control of the Persians politically. Ezra recognized that God's goodness to Israel, represented in the return to the land, was scarcely the fulfillment of all that was promised. And thus he says that Israel was enslaved even when they were back in the land.

If we quickly scan the history of Israel up until the time of Jesus and Paul, the same situation obtained. Israel enjoyed a brief time of freedom from about 164 BC to 63 BC under the Hasmoneans, but for much of the second and third centuries BC they were subjugated to either the Ptolemies or the Seleucids. Then in the middle of the first century BC the Romans took over Israel and appointed Herod the Great (39–4 BC) as the client king of Rome. N. T. Wright has famously argued, therefore, that Israel was still in exile under the Romans.[8] Scholars have debated

---

8   N. T. Wright, *The New Testament and the People of God*, vol. 1 of *Christian Origins and the Question of God* (Minneapolis: Fortress, 1992), 221–23, 371–417.

intensely whether Wright's describing Israel's situation as being under exile is justified.[9] Even if the term *exile* isn't the most accurate in the eyes of some, the substance of what Wright is saying is correct. The promises made to Israel had not yet been realized. Israel was waiting for the day when God would right all wrongs, judge the pagan nations, and bring in a king (the Messiah, see Pss. Sol. 17–18) who would reign over his people. The last line is a bit too simple because there were various conceptions about the Messiah present in Second Temple Judaism, but virtually all Jews looked forward to a glorious day when the promises made to Israel would be realized. And most agreed during the days of Jesus and Paul that the promises had not yet been fulfilled. In that sense, then, Israel was not yet free. Or to use the words of Ezra, they were still slaves.

We need to keep the history of Israel in mind when considering the message of Galatians. Those who attach themselves to the torah are "under a curse" (Gal. 3:10), "under sin" (3:22), "under the law" (3:23; 4:4; 5:18), "under a guardian" (3:25), "under the elements of the world" (4:3 CSB). As those who were under the law they were enslaved to sin, subjugated to its power and authority. In the allegory of the two sons, one of the sons is a slave and the other is free (4:22–26; 4:29–5:1), and the son who is enslaved lives under the old covenant, the Sinai covenant, the covenant with the stipulations of the law. Now however, with the coming of Jesus into the world "the fullness of time" has arrived (4:4). The promise the Lord made to Israel and the world that all peoples everywhere would be blessed through Abraham (Gal. 3:6–9, 14) was now realized. Abraham was promised land, offspring, and universal blessing (Gen. 12:1–3; 17:6–8; 18:18; 22:17–18). Paul identifies the offspring, the one true offspring of Abraham, as Jesus himself (Gal. 3:16). The pathway for receiving Abraham's blessing is only through Jesus, and mere ethnic descendance from Abraham doesn't qualify. Freedom is only realized through the Son whom God sent into the world as a

---

9   See, e.g., James M. Scott, ed., *Exile: A Conversation with N. T. Wright* (Downers Grove, IL: IVP Academic, 2017); Mark A. Seifrid, "Blind Alleys in the Controversy over the Paul of History," *TynBul* 45 (1994): 86–92.

human being (Gal. 4:4). Jesus was "born under the law, to redeem those who were under the law" (4:4–5) The word "redeem" (*exagorasē*), which is used only occasionally in English anymore, connotes freedom and liberation. Actually, the best term might be the word "ransom" since the freedom believers enjoy has come at a cost of Jesus's life that he sacrificed for the sake of his people.

God's apocalyptic act in Christ Jesus means freedom, and freedom is closely tied to the truth of the gospel, as we see in Galatians 2:3–5 and 2:11–14. The false brothers (2:4) and Peter (2:14) tried to compel (*anankazō*) Gentile believers to be circumcised. The former did so intentionally, and the latter unintentionally. In both instances Paul says they were threatening "the truth of the gospel" (2:5, 14), and Paul emphasizes that the truth of the gospel means freedom, while the antagonists were calling the Galatians back to slavery (2:4). The freedom in view is freedom from the curse of the law, which is achieved through Jesus's death (3:13), and Paul again uses the verb "redeem" (*exagorazō*) to describe the effect of Jesus's death. Another way to put it is that formerly, before being ransomed, believers were dead (2:19). The law didn't bring freedom but death. Nevertheless, those who have died with Christ are alive (2:19–20), due to the greatest apocalyptic act in history—the death of Christ. Those who are righteous "live by faith" rather than by relying on the law (3:11).

Another way of talking about freedom from slavery is to say that now believers are adopted in God's family; they are his sons and daughters. Those who are ransomed are no longer "under the law" but are God's adopted children (Gal. 4:5), which is another way of saying that the apocalyptic action of God in Christ has freed believers from bondage. As 4:7 declares, "You are no longer a slave, but a son, and if a son, then an heir through God." Or in 3:26, Paul emphasizes that "in Christ Jesus" all are God's sons and daughters through faith.

That brings up another polarity, or what J. Louis Martyn calls an antimony, that has been cancelled through the coming of Christ. Now the opposition between Jews and Gentiles, males and females, slaves and free has been erased (Gal. 3:28). The old polarities have come crashing down in Christ. Jews aren't prized over Gentiles; males aren't more significant than females; and masters aren't more important than slaves. All are "one" in Christ. We have to be careful, however, of misreading the verse as well. Paul isn't denying that there are Jews and Gentiles, males and females, masters and slaves. Redemption doesn't nullify creation, as if there were no differences at all, say, between males and females. Still, what Paul teaches is amazingly revolutionary and something almost all people in the ancient world didn't believe. Women and men are equally made in the image of God, and they have equal access to salvation. The same applies to Jews and Gentiles, and slaves and free. I will pick up the significance of the inclusion of the Gentiles in chapter 7, but we see that Paul breaks down barriers of ethnicity, gender, and class that have divided human beings for centuries.

Justification as Eschatological

In many instances when Paul uses the term "justify," he describes an already accomplished reality for believers. For instance, believers "have been justified by faith" (Rom. 5:1). Or "we have now been justified by his blood" (Rom. 5:9). We read in Romans 8:30, "Those whom he called he also justified, and those whom he justified he also glorified." First Corinthians 6:11 sounds a similar note: "You were justified in the name of the Lord Jesus Christ and by the Spirit of our God." Most of the texts in Galatians aren't clear about the time of justification, but it is probably fair to conclude that the idea is that one is already justified.

Thus, in Galatians 2:16 Paul declares, "We know that a person is not justified by works of the law but through faith in Jesus Christ, so we also have believed in Christ Jesus, in order to be justified by faith in Christ and not by works of the law, because by works of the law no one will be justified." The most natural way to read this is that those who put their faith in Christ are now declared to be in the right before God. The same reading is likely the case in the following texts: "And the Scripture, foreseeing that God would justify the Gentiles by faith" (3:8). "No one is justified before God by the law" (3:11). "So then, the law was our guardian until Christ came, in order that we might be justified by faith" (3:24). "You who are trying to be justified by the law are alienated from Christ" (5:4 CSB).

The desire to be justified in Galatians 2:17 could refer to final justification, but it isn't completely clear. "But if we ourselves are also found to be 'sinners' while seeking to be justified by Christ, is Christ then a promoter of sin?" (2:17 CSB). Still, there is one case where the noun "righteousness" is almost certainly eschatological.[10] "For through the Spirit, by faith, we ourselves eagerly wait for the hope of righteousness" (5:5). Since Paul speaks of eagerly waiting and of hope, the most plausible rendering is that he speaks of the final declaration of righteousness on the day of judgment. On that final day the Lord will declare to the world that those who trust in Christ are righteous.

If we step outside of Galatians for a moment, we find another important text that links justification to eschatology. Jesus Christ was justified, or acquitted, when he was raised from the dead (1 Tim. 3:16).[11] The resurrection vindicated Jesus, demonstrating that he was truly the Messiah, that he wasn't a deluded messianic pretender. The judgment of Pilate and the religious leaders that Jesus was guilty was reversed by God at the resurrection, showing that he was in the right.

We will look at justification by faith further in chapter 5, but here I note that justification is fundamentally eschatological. When God declares believers are justified by faith, he is announcing in advance the verdict that will be declared on the last day. The end time has reached into the present time, and this eschatological declaration belongs to believers now because Jesus has been declared to be in the right by his death and resurrection. Since believers are in Christ, the verdict that has been pronounced in Christ Jesus is now theirs by faith.

---

10 Douglas J. Moo, *Galatians*, BECNT (Grand Rapids, MI: Baker, 2013), 327–28; A. Andrew Das, *Galatians*, ConcC (St. Louis: Concordia, 2014), 528–29.
11 See G. K. Beale, "The Role of the Resurrection in the Already-and-Not-Yet Phases of Justification," in *For the Fame of God's Name: Essays in Honor of John Piper*, ed. Sam Storms and Justin Taylor (Wheaton, IL: Crossway, 2010), 190–213.

Conclusion

The apocalyptic and eschatological character of Paul's theology is stitched into the warp and woof of Galatians. It surfaces in Paul's emphasis on the new creation, the new age that has dawned in Jesus Christ. The old creation is passing away and the new era has now come in Jesus Christ. Jesus's resurrection indicates that the new age has arrived, one where there is life rather than death, blessing instead of curse, joy instead of sorrow. The giving of the Spirit also betokens the fulfillment of God's end-time promises. The pouring out of the Spirit means that the new exodus has now come. Believers are no longer subjugated to the flesh but live in the new era of the Spirit. The Spirit–flesh contrast fits as well with the contrast between freedom and slavery. Slavery characterizes the old age, particularly in terms of subjugation to sin. God's apocalyptic act of deliverance and redemption in Christ frees and liberates those who belong to Jesus. Now they are free to live the way God intended people to live since true freedom expresses itself in obedience. Finally, justification is eschatological as well since the declaration that those who trust in Christ Jesus are right before God represents God's end-time verdict. When believers are justified, however, that verdict is pronounced in advance. Through the death and resurrection of Christ, the eschaton has now penetrated the present evil age, and thus believers receive God's verdict on their lives before the final day of judgment.

4

Circumcision and the Cross

Introduction

One of the striking eschatological/apocalyptic polarities in Galatians shows up in Paul's understanding of the cross and circumcision. The cross and circumcision represent two different pathways into the people of God. We have seen that the typical Jewish view required circumcision for entry into the people of God. To put it another way: one had to be circumcised to be in covenant with God, and for those who were from a Gentile background, circumcision was mandated for them to become proselytes. Paul, on the other hand, presented a stark alternative. If one insisted on circumcision for conversion, then one denied the efficacy of the cross. Since the new age has arrived apocalyptically in Jesus, then Christ's death (not circumcision!) is the means by which one becomes part of the people of God. When I refer to the cross in this chapter, I am not limiting myself to places where the word "cross" is used. Instead under the rubric "cross" I am including any reference to Christ's death. It is quite striking how the cross plays such a decisive role in the letter, indicating that the new era has commenced with the cross and resurrection of Jesus.

The Cross Begins and Ends the Letter

The radical opposition between circumcision and the cross is implied when we compare Galatians 5:3 with 2:21. In the former verse, the acceptance of circumcision indicates that one "is obligated to keep the whole law" (5:3). This likely means that one must accept the entire law to be saved. By way of contrast, Paul declares in 2:21 that "if righteousness were through the law, then Christ died for no purpose." The word "righteousness" here refers to right-standing with God, to a right relationship with him. If one takes upon oneself the law in order to obtain righteousness, then the first step—the sign that one was under the law—was submitting to circumcision. Conversely, if one trusts in Christ, the law isn't required for entrance into the people of God. Indeed, if the law suffices, then Christ's death is superfluous since circumcision and observance of the law qualify to bring one into God's presence. Since God sent Christ to die to secure salvation, it follows that circumcision can't be the means by which access to God is obtained. The death of Christ hoists a banner over the torah, proclaiming that it isn't the way to God. Christ didn't die in vain. He died to secure righteousness for those who trust in him. He died to bring human beings into a right relation with God. If people turn to circumcision or anything else besides Christ, they end up saying in effect that Christ died for nothing.

The significance of Christ's death is signaled early in the letter where Paul says that Jesus "gave himself for our sins to deliver us from the present evil age" (Gal. 1:4). I examined this verse earlier, but here it should be noted that the verse is in the introduction to the letter (1:1–5), and this is the *only* letter written by Paul where Christ's death is mentioned in the introductory greeting. The reference to Christ's death, then, is of massive importance, showing the centrality of the cross in the letter. Jesus died to rescue believers from "the present evil age," and as noted earlier we have exodus themes in this verse. If we read Galatians 1:4 in light of the rest of the letter, the Galatians—by considering circumcision—were in danger of falling back into the clutches of the present evil era. The new age had dawned, and the Galatian Christians needed to realize afresh the significance of the cross. A new world order had commenced with Jesus's death, and the Galatians were in danger of stepping back, so to speak, in time. We could say that they were on the precipice of returning to earth after being introduced spiritually into heaven's realms.

The theme of the cross functions as an inclusio in the letter. It isn't limited to the introduction but also surfaces in Paul's conclusion: "But far be it from me to boast except in the cross of our Lord Jesus Christ, by which the world has been crucified to me, and I to the world" (Gal. 6:14). The context here is suggestive, for in 6:12–13 Paul criticizes the antagonists, charging that they were promoting circumcision to avoid being "persecuted for the cross of Christ" (6:12). Paul indicts the motives of his opponents. Their devotion to circumcision was self-protective; their religion was a cover for their own selfish desires and way of life. They may have looked religious, but it was a front for another agenda. Actually, Paul informs us, they did not even keep the law themselves. Their evil way of life was evident if one examined them impartially. Nor did they truly care about the Galatians. They wanted to add the Galatians as their disciples so that they could boast about their influence. Their piety was a pretense for advancing their own agenda, for an idolatrous and narcissistic self-regard. They weren't concerned about the world to come but with this world, this era, this evil age, their own reputations.

If we consider Galatians 6:12–14, circumcision is confined to this world, just as it is consigned to the present age in 1:4. Circumcision is advocated by Paul's adversaries to avoid the scandal of the cross, and curiously enough the agitators falsely charged Paul, claiming that he preached and practiced circumcision in other contexts (Gal. 5:11). Circumcision—which is demanded for salvation by the agitators—is, according to Paul, worldly and contrary to the new creation (Gal. 6:15). The cross announces to the world the spiritual poverty of the human being. Revelation 3:17 describes the human condition, even if the context is different, for the cross declares that we are "wretched, pitiable, poor, blind, and naked." What we need as human beings, then, is crucifixion, for the only pathway to life is death.

Galatians 6:17 reflects the same standpoint: "From now on let no one cause me trouble, for I bear on my body the marks of Jesus." The opponents criticized Paul relentlessly, claiming that he was not pleasing to God since he didn't preach the necessity of circumcision to the Galatians. But if they thought Paul was doing this to avoid persecution and prosecution, they were deluding themselves since the marks on Paul's body were inflicted (at least in part) by synagogue authorities. We are told in 2 Corinthians 11:24 that Paul was whipped with thirty-nine lashes five times—a Jewish punishment that accords with the torah (see Deut. 25:3). Since Paul had been in ministry at least fifteen years by the time he wrote Galatians, some of these beatings were inflicted on him by the time he wrote Galatians. Paul refers to "the physical wounds and scars left on his body as a result of the various sufferings he experienced as an apostle."[1] The agitators were obsessed with circumcision, but Paul reminds his readers that the marks on his body were inflicted because of his devotion to Jesus Christ as the crucified one. It is fascinating that Paul uses the word "bear" (*bastazō*) for the marks that he received on his body. Luke uses the same word when Jesus commands his disciples to carry the cross daily (Luke 14:27). In the Gospel of John we find the same verb as John records Jesus carrying his cross on the road to Golgotha (John 19:17). The marks on Paul's body were his credentials, verifying that he was a true apostle, that he was willing even to die for Christ's sake, that he was (so to speak) carrying his cross, and that he no longer lived to please people but Christ alone.

Understanding the Meaning of the Cross

Paul unpacks the meaning of Christ's death for believers in Galatians 2:19–20, using the first person pronoun "I" so that his life functions as the paradigm for the life of believers. The meaning of the words "through the law I died to the law" (2:19) isn't instantly clear. It could mean that death comes because of sin, because we fail to keep God's commands found in the law.[2] This interpretation is quite plausible, especially because we find this theme elsewhere in Paul (Rom. 7:5–25;

---

[1] Jeffrey A. D. Weima, "Gal 6:11–18: A Hermeneutical Key to the Galatian Letter," *CTJ* 28 (1993): 98.

[2] E.g, Gordon D. Fee, *Galatians*, Pentecostal Commentary (Dorset: Deo, 2007), 91.

1 Cor. 15:56). I incline, however, to seeing a parallel with Galatians 2:20 where the "I" died at Christ's death, meaning that believers died at Christ's crucifixion since they were crucified with Christ. Christ's death transcends time so that his death becomes the death of believers when they come to faith. Thus, upon coming to faith in Christ believers die to the law since they have died with Christ.[3] The parallel with Romans 7:4 supports the interpretation favored here: "You also have died to the law through the body of Christ." The redemptive-historical and apocalyptic significance of Christ's death comes to the forefront, for the era of the law, which leads to the death of human beings, has ended with the death and resurrection of Christ. Accepting circumcision, therefore, is not the solution to the human predicament but the problem! What we need isn't another commandment but death and resurrection, and these have become a reality in Jesus.

The significance of Christ's death is heralded in Galatians 3:1, as Paul continues to try to impress on believers the centrality of the cross. The Galatians had been bewitched and dazzled, as if someone had cast a spell over them. It is likely that the Galatians' enchantment was the work of Satan, who had turned their eyes away from Christ's cross.[4] Instead of thinking about what Christ had accomplished for them, they wanted to perform the works of the law to be right before God (3:2, 5). They had begun to believe that their own activity, their own righteousness, would qualify them to stand before God. In doing this they were imitating Peter (2:11–14), who came perilously close to denying the truth of the gospel.[5] Thus, in 3:1–5 Paul brings the Galatians back to the days of their conversion, to the days when they heard Paul proclaim the gospel of Christ crucified and risen. The Galatians' reversal since then was nothing short of shocking and astonishing to Paul. They were hesitating because they were listening to the wrong

---

3 So Richard B. Hays, *The Letter to the Galatians: Introduction, Commentary, and Reflections*, vol. 11 of *The New Interpreter's Bible* (Nashville: Abingdon, 2000), 243.

4 See Jerome H. Neyrey, "Bewitched in Galatia: Paul and Cultural Anthropology," *CBQ* 50 (1988): 72–100.

5 Walter G. Hansen, *Abraham in Galatians: Epistolary and Rhetorical Context*, JSNTSup 29 (Sheffield: Sheffield Academic Press, 1989), 109.

messages and needed to be recalled afresh to the world-shaking impact of the cross. To the extent that they were attracted to the works of the law, to the same extent the meaning of the cross was slipping, so to speak, through their fingers.

Paul's emphasis on Christ crucified raises the question as to the meaning of the cross, for we need to understand why Paul believed the cross was decisive for the salvation of human beings. Paul explicates in Galatians 3:13 and 4:4–5 what was achieved in Christ's death. In particular, human beings were redeemed and freed through the death of Christ. In both 3:13 and 4:5, Paul uses the verb "redeem" (*exagorazō*), and the word denotes God purchasing his people from the realm of evil. Jesus's redeeming work means freedom, freedom from sin and freedom from death. Redemption reaches back to exodus where God delivered or freed his people from Egyptian slavery (e.g., Ex. 6:6; 15:13; Deut. 7:8; 9:26; 13:5; 15:15; 21:8; 24:18), but the redemption accomplished by Jesus is even greater since he frees people from the most insidious slavery of all—slavery to sin. Isaiah picks up redemption language and describes it as a second exodus where God will once again free Israel—this time from Babylonian exile (Isa. 11:15–16; 40:3–11; 42:16; 43:2, 5–7, 16–19; 49:6–11; 51:10). But if we examine Isaiah at a deeper level we see that Israel was in exile because of its sin and iniquity (e.g., Isa. 40:2; 42:17, 20, 24–25; 43:22–24). When we think of redemption, we should also think of the social world that Paul and his contemporaries inhabited where slaves could be manumitted (freed!) through the payment of a price. Both the Hebrew and Greek backgrounds point forward to the great redemption accomplished by Jesus at the cross where he freed and liberated from sin those who belong to him.

In Galatians 3:13 Paul explains how redemption works, painting in bold colors how Jesus freed, liberated, and redeemed believers from the curse pronounced on all people because of the law. Those under the law are cursed not because the law is evil or Satanic but because of human fallenness, because human beings fail to do what the law commands, which is another way of saying that we are cursed because of disobedience and sin. Those who are cursed (cf. Gal. 1:8–9) will face God's judgment. Human beings, then, find themselves in quite a predicament since they are cursed for transgressions and iniquity, and there is no way the evil we have done can be reversed through our own efforts. Thankfully, Jesus removes the curse from those who belong to him because he took their curse upon himself. He was cursed "for us [*hyper hēmōn*]" (3:13). We have a clear example here of substitution since Jesus took upon himself the curse that human beings deserved. Indeed, it is right to speak of penal substitution since he received the penalty (the curse) that sinners deserved. He died the death we should have died and, thereby, freed believers from the dominion of sin. We can rightly say that Christ's death is both substitutionary and an example of *Christus Victor*. It is substitutionary in that Christ died in the place of sinners and took the curse we deserved. On the other hand, the theme of *Christus Victor* is also present since the chains of slavery have been broken, and those redeemed are free. Through the cross, both the curse and the dominion of sin have been dethroned.

Paul quotes Deuteronomy 21:23 in Galatians 3:13 to support the idea that Jesus was cursed on the cross. Peter Craigie explains well the meaning of Deuteronomy 21:23 in its historical context:

> Hanging was not a method of execution, but something that was done after the death of a criminal, on the same day. When the man was dead, he would be hanged on a *tree* or a "wooden post" of some kind; the gruesome sight would then serve as a warning to the population of the results of breaking those laws which were punishable by death.[6]

By the Second Temple period (roughly 400 BC to AD 200) the text was also applied to those who were crucified (cf. 4QpNah 5-8; 11QTemple 64.6-13).[7] The Old Testament significance of hanging on a tree, then, applies to Jesus, but he wasn't cursed for his own sin and evil. He was

---

6 Peter C. Craigie, *The Book of Deuteronomy*, NICOT (Grand Rapids, MI: Eerdmans, 1976), 285.
7 See Joseph A. Fitzmyer, "Crucifixion in Ancient Palestine, Qumran Literature, and the NT," *CBQ* 40 (1978): 493-513.

cursed "for us," for our sake and for our salvation. Jesus took upon himself the curse that his people deserved, and in doing so he freed them forever.

The cross of Jesus plays a massive role in Paul's theology because human evil cannot be overturned any other way. Nor is the case that the law, even the sacrifices offered to bring about forgiveness, could ultimately bring atonement.[8] If these sacrifices could atone, then Christ died for nothing (Gal. 2:21). Forgiveness and freedom could never be achieved finally through the offering of animals. Instead, these animal sacrifices were temporary, pointing forward to and finding their fulfillment in Christ's cross. The cross of Christ, not circumcision or any other part of the law, is the gateway by which the curse that comes from sin is lifted so that believers enjoy fellowship with God. The Galatians, if they tacked back to circumcision, would cancel the effect of the cross in their lives.

The redemptive work of Christ is also featured in Galatians 4:4–5. The "fullness of time" (Gal. 4:4; cf. Mark 1:15; Eph. 1:10) dawned with the coming of Jesus Christ, and God's purposes in redemption were being realized with the coming of the Messiah. We have an indication here that the cross is both apocalyptic and salvation-historical. With the death and resurrection of Jesus "the end of the ages has come" (1 Cor. 10:11). Jesus came at the time designated by God (Gal. 4:2) as one sent by God (4:4), fulfilling the ancient promises. God's covenant promises were fulfilled with the arrival of the long-awaited Messiah. At the same time, we have an apocalyptic act since God invaded history in a surprising and climactic way. We have a fulfillment that occurred in a dramatic manner, an invasion that shattered the rule of demonic powers and dethroned the authority of sin and death.

Since Jesus was sent by God, he preexisted inasmuch as God could not send one who did not yet exist. Thus, Jesus being sent certifies his deity. At the same time, being born of woman focuses on his humanity. We shouldn't read the virgin birth into the expression, for Job 25:4 speaks of one "born of woman," describing the birth of a human being

---

8 See A. Andrew Das, *Paul, the Law, and the Covenant* (Peabody, MA: Hendrickson, 2001), 144.

(cf. also Matt 11:11; Job 14:1; 15:14; Josephus, *Ant.* 7.21; 16.382). Thus the phrase points to Jesus's full humanity. Jesus Christ, then, in accordance with the ancient creeds—Chalcedon in particular—was fully God and fully man. As human beings we could only be redeemed by one who was both divine and human.

Jesus came as one "born under the law, to redeem those who were under the law" (Gal. 4:4–5). Jesus is the exception that proves the rule since he is the only person who lived under the law who was free from sin. The law, as we shall see in chapter 6, is closely aligned with sin, and all those under the law are also under sin. Life under the law is likened to being under the elements of the world, to being a slave (Gal. 4:3). Even though Jesus lived under the law, he wasn't enslaved to the elements, nor was he under the curse of sin. He always lived as God's obedient Son.[9] He freed, liberated, and ransomed those who were enslaved to the elements of the world. His coming shattered with an apocalyptic act of power the fetters that bound human beings. Jesus means freedom, but that freedom came at the cost of his life through the death on the cross. We should also note that what was accomplished at the cross is not limited to freedom from slavery. Believers are also adopted as God's sons and daughters (cf. Rom. 8:15, 23; 9:4; Eph. 1:5). Now all believers, both Jewish and Gentile, are part of the family of God, deeply loved and cherished by God, children in whom he finds delight. As Trevor Burke remarks, "God's family comprises solely adopted sons and daughters—there are no natural-born sons or daughters in his divine household."[10]

A true understanding of the cross also explains the severe and uncompromising rejection of circumcision in Galatians 5:2–4. One either benefits from circumcision or from Christ, from the law or the cross, from human achievement or divine grace. Even though the cross isn't mentioned in these verses, the reference to Christ pulls us into the orbit of the cross. If one truly puts trust in Christ and him crucified, then

---

9 So Richard N. Longenecker, *Galatians*, WBC (Dallas: Word, 1990), 171–72.

10 Trevor J. Burke, *Adoption into God's Family: Exploring a Pauline Metaphor*, NSBT 22 (Downers Grove, IL: InterVarsity Press, 2006), 89.

one will not turn to the law or circumcision to be right with God. The cross is inextricably tied together with grace, with God's saving action in Christ Jesus. The cross of Jesus heralds to the world that salvation and freedom for human beings is a divine work. Human ingenuity, human virtue, human strength can't provide what is needed.

Conclusion

Two options stand before the Galatians: circumcision or the cross—the law or grace—human performance or the saving work of God in Christ. Paul argues that those who have known the saving and redeeming work of Christ through the cross have been freed from the curse of sin and are now adopted as God's sons and daughters. The law leads to frustration, failure, and finally to death. The only pathway to the new creation is death and resurrection. True redemption is God's work and can't be accomplished through human beings, and thus the cross reminds the Galatians that salvation is of the Lord. Jesus defeated the powers at his death and also died in the place of sinners, taking the curse upon himself that human beings deserved.

5

Justification by Faith

Introduction

The letter to the Galatians, like the epistle to the Romans, is well-known for its discussion of justification. It is instructive that justification and righteousness are particularly emphasized in contexts where opponents insist that one must observe the law in order to be saved. Galatians isn't alone in this regard, for we see an emphasis on law-observance in Romans (Rom. 3:27–4:25) and Philippians (Phil. 3:2–11) as well. The apocalyptic school tends to understand righteousness in transformative terms. In other words, justification signals that one is made righteous by the powerful grace of God.[1] God's righteousness is also understood to be his covenant faithfulness, and in N. T. Wright's case justification centers on ecclesiology (covenant membership) instead of soteriology so that the focus is horizontal instead of vertical.[2] Justification isn't, according to this latter interpretation, so much about how to be right with God but centers on right relationships with one another. I will argue that

---

1 Ernst Käsemann, "God's Righteousness in Paul," *Journal of Theology and Church* 1 (1965): 100–110; Peter Stuhlmacher, "The Apostle Paul's View of Righteousness," in *Reconciliation, Law and Righteousness: Essays in Biblical Theology* (Philadelphia: Fortress, 1986), 68–93.
2 N. T. Wright, *What Saint Paul Really Said: Was Paul of Tarsus the Real Founder of Christianity?* (Grand Rapids, MI: Eerdmans, 1997), 120, 125, 133; N. T. Wright, *Justification: God's Plan and Paul's Vision* (Downers Grove, IL: InterVarsity Press, 2010), 116, 131–34.

both the apocalyptic interpretation and the ecclesiological reading proposed by Wright are off-center and that there is a better way to understand the term.

Justification Is Forensic

Against the apocalyptic interpretation, I will argue that justification is forensic instead of being transformative. Certainly Paul teaches that Christians are transformed by God's grace, as we shall see particularly in chapter 8. But we must not make the mistake of reading Paul's theology as a whole into every word he uses. Salvation has many dimensions (redemption, reconciliation, sanctification, etc.), but the terms don't all mean the same thing. We should not merge the words together so that justification means the same thing as sanctification. We could, of course, make the mistake of driving too sharp a wedge between the various words Paul uses to describe our salvation in Christ. But at the same time we could make the mistake of lumping words together indiscriminately so that they lose their distinct meanings.

It is also a mistake to collapse covenant and righteousness together in Paul. Actually, Paul rarely puts the two words "righteousness" and "covenant" together.[3] Now we should not conclude from this that covenant is a minor theme in Paul, nor should we conclude that righteousness has nothing to do with covenant. Still, since the words aren't collocated together, we have significant evidence that covenant isn't the dominant lens by which we should define justification. If we think broadly, we could say that God's righteousness fulfills God's covenant promises, but that isn't the same thing as saying that God's righteousness *is* covenant faithfulness.

We should begin by looking at the meaning of the verb "justify" (*dikaioō*), and what is striking is that the verb is clearly forensic, that it has to do with being declared righteous instead of being

---

3 This case is made especially in the important book by Mark A. Seifrid, *Christ, Our Righteousness: Paul's Theology of Justification*, NSBT 9 (Downers Grove, IL: InterVarsity Press, 2001).

made righteous. A few examples should make this clear.⁴ We read in Deuteronomy 25:1, "If there is a dispute between men and they come into court and the judges decide between them, acquitting [*dikaiōsōsin*] the innocent and condemning the guilty." Judges don't *make* the righteous innocent; they declare them to be such on the basis of the evidence presented in court. We find a similar example in 1 Kings 8:32 (cf. 2 Chron. 6:23) where Solomon is praying, asking God to "judge your servants, condemning the guilty by bringing his conduct on his own head, and vindicating [*dikaiōsai*] the righteous by rewarding him according to his righteousness." Solomon isn't asking God in this context to *make* those who are wicked righteous. He asks God to judge righteously, to render judgment according to what they have done so that the wicked are declared to be guilty and the righteous are declared to be innocent. Elihu exhorts Job,

> If you have any words, answer me;
> speak, for I desire to justify [*dikaiōthēnai*] you. (Job 33:32)

Elihu is saying that he wants the court of public opinion to realize that Job is in the right. Elihu is certainly not saying that he wants to *make* Job righteous. Instead, he wants to show that Job stands in the right, that there is no basis for condemning him.

The forensic character of righteousness is a common theme. Isaiah speaks out about the wickedness in Israel, calling them back to justice, saying, "bring justice [*dikaiōsate*] to the fatherless" (Isa. 1:17). Justice is to be enacted, to be made a reality in the public sphere. Still, it is a confusion of terms to conclude from this that the verb means "make righteous." The justice that orphans deserve is being flouted in society, and thus the righteousness that belongs to orphans should be enforced by judges. The judges aren't making anyone righteous, but they are enshrining and implementing justice in the political sphere.

---

4 Although the following quotations from the ESV Old Testament are based on the MT, I have provided the form of *dikaioō* that appears in the LXX.

The legal character of righteousness shines forth as well when the Lord says,

> Put me in remembrance; let us argue together;
> set forth your case, that you may be proved right [*dikaiōthēs*]."
> (Isa. 43:26; cf. also Isa. 43:9)

The Lord invites Israel to go to court with him and to argue their case in court. There it will be evident if their case is truly right. It isn't envisioned that a judge would *make Israel right*. Quite the contrary. The question is whether they are declared to be in the right in their lawsuit against the Lord.

Paul also regularly uses the verb with a forensic meaning. For instance, Romans 2:13 says, "The doers of the law . . . will be justified [*dikaiōthēsontai*]." The legal and declarative sense of the verb is evident since those who keep the law will be declared to be in the right by the divine judge on the last day. They will not be made right but declared to be in the right. Or consider Romans 3:4,

> That you may be justified [*dikaiōthēs*] in your words,
> and triumph when you judge. (CSB)

Paul explains that when God judges sin, he is vindicated and shown to be in the right since those judged have flouted his will. The legal character of justification is also clear in Romans 8:33, "Who shall bring any charge against God's elect? It is God who justifies [*dikaiōn*]." We have a law court context where God as the judge declares that those who are his own—the elect, his people—are in the right before him. No charge of guilt will stand.

The legal dimension of righteousness also surfaces in 1 Corinthians 4:4: "For I am not aware of anything against myself, but I am not thereby acquitted [*dedikaiōmai*]. It is the Lord who judges me." Paul considers the verdict he will receive from the Lord on the day of judgment, informing the Corinthians that it is the Lord, as the divine judge, who will declare him to be in the right and vindicate him. Another fascinating text speaks to the justification of Christ himself:

> He was manifested in the flesh,
>   vindicated [*edikaiōthē*] by the Spirit. (1 Tim. 3:16)

The vindication referred to occurred at Jesus's resurrection, showing that he was not condemned by God. Jesus's crucifixion suggested to people that God rejected him as a lawbreaker and blasphemer. They reasoned that God would not have allowed Jesus to die in such a horrible way if he were truly righteous. By way of contrast, Jesus's resurrection demonstrates that he was approved by God, that he was declared to be in the right before God. God did not *make* Jesus righteous at the resurrection but declared him to be in the right, publicly vindicating him.

When we investigate the word "justify" in Galatians, it should be interpreted according to this legal frame. Three times in Galatians 2:16 we are told that people are justified (*dikaioō*) by faith in Jesus Christ instead of via the works of the law. Human beings don't stand in the right before God because of their adherence to the torah but through faith in Jesus. The word "justified" has a declarative sense here, and the next verse indicates why works of the law don't justify: "But if, in our endeavor to be justified [*dikaiōthēnai*] in Christ, we too were found to be sinners, is Christ then a servant of sin? Certainly not!" (Gal. 2:17). The Lord, as the divine judge, declares that people are not right before him by the works of torah. The word "found" (*heuriskō*) often has a legal and judicial sense (see Acts 4:21; 13:28; 23:9, 29; 24:5, 12, 20; Rom. 4:1; 1 Cor. 4:2; 15:15; 2 Cor. 12:20; Phil. 3:9; 2 Tim. 1:18; 1 Pet. 1:7; 2 Pet. 3:10, 14; Rev. 2:2; 14:5; 20:15), and that is the case in Galatians 2:17 as well. The reason for their condemnation is disobedience: people are "found to be sinners"—declared to be sinners—by the law. Thus, they will not stand in the right before God by their obedience since they are sinners. Instead they are right before God by faith. Paul reiterates these same themes several times in Galatians, affirming that justification is by faith (Gal. 3:8, 24) and not via the law (3:11; 5:4).

I have argued that the verb "justify" has a forensic sense in Galatians 2:16–17, but what should we make of the noun "righteousness" (*dikaiosynē*) in 2:21? "I do not nullify the grace of God, for if righteousness were through the law, then Christ died for no purpose." Does the noun "righteousness" also have a forensic meaning? It seems unlikely that the verb "justify" and the noun "righteousness" should be assigned different meanings since they both occur in the same context and they also address the same subject matter—that is, whether human beings can stand in the right before God.

The same conclusion should be drawn regarding the use of the word "righteousness" in Galatians 3:6. Paul refers to Abraham who "believed God, and it was counted to him as righteousness." Possibly, we could understand Paul to be saying that Abraham's faith was virtuous, and if this is the case, then "righteousness" would stand for Abraham's righteousness, his ethical virtue. Such a reading, however, contradicts the message of Galatians as a whole since *God's grace* saves—not the righteousness of human beings. This is confirmed when we read Galatians 3:2 and 3:5 where faith is opposed to works of the law. In the same way, then, in 3:6 faith and human works represent two different approaches to God. Interestingly, in 3:8, which is only two verses after 3:6, Paul declares that "Scripture" foresaw "that God would justify the Gentiles by faith." The noun "righteousness" and the verb "justify" are closely aligned. We have already seen that the verb is forensic, and it makes sense that the noun "righteousness" should be understood similarly. In both 3:6 and 3:8, belief is necessary to be right with God.

The noun "righteousness" is also found in Galatians 3:21, and it should be read forensically as well: "Is the law then contrary to the promises of God? Certainly not! For if a law had been given that could give life, then righteousness would indeed be by the law." If we consider how closely 3:21 reflects 3:11, the legal and declarative sense of justification finds further support. We see in 3:11 the close connection between the verb "justify" and the verb "live," and in 3:21 the noun "righteousness" is connected with the verb "live." The point here isn't that the words "justify" and "live" have the same meaning. The two words aren't synonyms. The aim is to show that the verb "justify" and the noun "righteousness" are both declarative, emphasizing that the law doesn't justify or bring righteousness. So, it is very unlikely that the noun "righteousness" (*dikaiosynē*) and the verb "justify" (*dikaioō*) have different meanings. In both instances, one's right standing before God is in view.

The last use of the noun "righteousness" appears in Galatians 5:5: "For through the Spirit, by faith, we ourselves eagerly wait for the hope of righteousness." It is certainly possible that the reference here is to ethical righteousness. But the uses of the term thus far in the letter and the context point to a forensic understanding. Galatians 5:4 refers to those who are trying to "be justified by the law," and the verb is clearly forensic. It seems quite unlikely that the noun "righteousness," which occurs in the next verse (5:5), has a different meaning than the verb "justify" in 5:4. The subject matter addressed also leads us to the same conclusion. Paul contrasts faith and the work of the Spirit with the law in 5:5, and by this point in the letter the notion that people stand in the right before God by faith is a common theme. There are good reasons, then, to conclude that on the last day God will declare publicly to the world that believers stand in the right before him. I conclude that in Galatians the noun "righteousness" has a forensic sense and that the noun "righteousness" and the verb "justify" should not be distinguished from each other in meaning.

Justification Is Fundamentally Soteriological

Another implication of the use of the word "justify" should be noted. When Paul uses the verb, he regularly contrasts, as we have just seen, being justified by faith with being justified by the law or by the works of the law. We learn from this that justification speaks to one's relationship with God since justification doesn't refer to standing in the right before people but before God. Thus, N. T. Wright's claim that justification is fundamentally ecclesiological is backwards because justification speaks of one's relationship with God. Further evidence for this contention is found in Galatians 3:11: "Now it is evident that no one is justified before God by the law, for 'The righteous shall live by faith.'" Paul directly speaks of being justified in God's sight. We should also notice that the first clause has the verb "justified," and the second the verb "shall live." These two verbs are alternate ways of describing the same reality. The verb "live" refers to life with reference to God, what John often describes as eternal life. Eternal life is a gift of God, confirming that the focus is vertical instead of being horizontal.

Galatians 3:21 constitutes further evidence for the notion that righteousness focuses on one's relationship with God: "Is the law then contrary to the promises of God? Certainly not! For if a law had been given that could give life, then righteousness would indeed be by the law." "Righteousness" and "life" are not synonyms here, but they are closely related. As in 3:11, life speaks of one's relationship with God, and thus there are good grounds for saying that righteousness speaks to one's relationship with God. Certainly there are ecclesiological and horizontal implications of justification, and in this sense we can find some agreement with Wright. Still, justification and life are fundamentally soteriological realities. Surprisingly, Wright reverses the emphasis of the text because the evidence for seeing justification as having to do with covenant membership is actually quite limited. It seems rather obvious, however, that it has to do with one's relationship with God.

Faith in Jesus, Not the Law

Paul teaches that justification is by faith instead of by observing the law. Human beings are declared to be right before God by virtue of faith in Jesus. Still, many scholars today argue that the Greek phrase *pistis Christou* should be translated as the "faithfulness of Christ" (a subjective genitive in Greek) instead of "faith in Christ" (an objective genitive).[5]

---

5 E.g., Richard B. Hays, *The Faith of Jesus Christ: An Investigation of the Narrative Substructure of Galatians 3:1–4:11*, 2nd ed. (Grand Rapids, MI: Eerdmans, 2002); Ian G. Wallis, *The Faith of Jesus Christ in Early Christian Traditions*, SNTSMS 84 (Cambridge: Cambridge University Press, 1995).

I think the traditional reading—"faith in Christ"—is still persuasive for the following reasons.[6]

1. We find other cases where a noun in the genitive is the object of faith. For instance, the most natural way to read Mark 11:22 is with the translation, "have faith in God" (*echete pistin theou*). James 2:1 should be understood in a similar way: "Show no partiality as you hold the faith in our Lord Jesus Christ [*echete tēn pistin tou kyriou hēmōn Iēsou Christou*], the Lord of glory." Jesus is clearly the object of faith in this verse. Since we see that God / Jesus (in the genitive case) is the object of faith in Mark and James, it is no surprise to say that Jesus or Christ (in the genitive case) is the object of faith in Paul.

2. Some scholars say reading the genitive as objective (faith *in Jesus*) doesn't fit with how Greek grammar works, but we have already seen that Mark and James use the genitive that way. And there are other places in Paul where genitives are objective with nouns that are comparable to "faith." For instance, 1 Thessalonians 1:3 refers to "hope in our Lord Jesus Christ" (*tēs elpidos tou kyriou hēmōn Iēsou Christou*). The noun "hope" is very close in meaning to "faith," and Paul is clearly not talking about the hopefulness of Jesus but *hope in Jesus*. If Jesus is the object of *hope* in a genitive phrase, then he can also be the object of *faith* in a genitive phrase. In the same way, Paul writes about "the knowledge of Christ Jesus [*tēs gnōseōs Christou Iēsou*]" (Phil. 3:8 KJV), and Christ in this context is clearly the object of knowledge.

---

[6] See Moisés Silva, "Faith Versus Works of Law in Galatians," in *The Paradoxes of Paul*, vol. 2 of *Justification and Variegated Nomism*, ed. D. A. Carson, Peter T. O'Brien, and Mark A. Seifrid (Grand Rapids, MI: Baker, 2004), 217–48; Barry Matlock, "Detheologizing the *PISTIS CHRISTOU* Debate: Cautionary Remarks from a Lexical Semantic Perspective," *NovT* 62 (2000): 1–23; Barry Matlock, "*PISTIS* in Galatians 3:26: Neglected Evidence for 'Faith in Christ'?," *NTS* 49 (2003): 433–39; Stanley E. Porter and Andrew W. Pitts, "*Pistis* with a Preposition and Genitive Modifier: Lexical, Semantic and Syntactic Considerations in the *Pistis Christou* Discussion," in *The Faith of Jesus Christ: Exegetical, Biblical, and Theological Studies*, ed. Michael F. Bird and Preston M. Sprinkle (Grand Rapids, MI: Baker Academic, 2010), 33–53; B. J. Oropeza, "Justification by Faith in Christ or Faithfulness of Christ? Updating the ΠΙΣΤΙΣ ΧΡΙΣΤΟΥ Debate in Light of Paul's Use of Scripture," *JTS* 72 (2021): 102–24.

3. In some texts the idea of believing in order to be justified sits next to faith in Jesus (e.g., Gal. 3:22). Some claim that Paul can't be talking about faith in Jesus in these cases because it would be redundant to speak of faith in Jesus *and* believing. But this objection misses the mark. Paul includes both faith in Jesus and believing for emphasis, stressing how important it is to believe to be justified.[7] We should also notice that the two expressions (believing and faith in Jesus) aren't exactly the same (see Rom. 3:22; Gal. 3:22; Phil. 3:9). They are not precise synonyms. Paul speaks of believing in general in one case and more specifically of *faith in Christ* in the other. The latter phrase is more explicit, reminding us that our faith is not a general diffuse faith but faith *in Jesus*.

4. Another piece of evidence supporting "faith in Christ" is the contrast between works of the law and faith in Jesus (e.g., Gal. 2:16). Paul contrasts *two human activities*, two human responses to God's revelation in Christ. One either believes in Jesus or one attempts to do the works required to be right with God.

5. Some think that Galatians 3:23-25 supports the "faithfulness of Christ" since we have the expression "faith came" (Gal. 3:23) and "now that faith has come" (3:25). We clearly have the notion of faith arriving at a specific time in redemptive history. It is not evident, however, that the reference to faith coming at a particular time in salvation history supports a subjective-genitive reading. It makes perfect sense to preserve the redemptive-historical sense of faith coming at a particular time in the history of salvation with the idea that the faith that has come is faith in Jesus. Before the coming of Jesus, faith wasn't directed particularly to him since he had not yet been revealed to the world. It is a false step to posit a dichotomy between salvation history / apocalyptic and anthropology. Salvation history and apocalyptic center on what God has done in Christ, but God's work also leads to a human response. We don't want to fall into a kind of hyper-Calvinism where God's work leaves human beings untouched. The human act of believ-

---

7 See Moisés Silva, *Biblical Words and Their Meaning: An Introduction to Lexical Semantics* (Grand Rapids, MI: Zondervan, 1983), 153–56. Silva sees the rule here of maximal redundancy.

ing in Jesus becomes a reality only after God intervenes in history in the person of Jesus.

6. Interestingly, Paul doesn't often use the word "faithful" to describe Christ's work for us. If he did, we might have more reason to think that the phrase under consideration refers to the "faithfulness of Christ." In fact, there is only one clear instance where Paul refers to Jesus's faithfulness (2 Tim. 2:13), and the syntax isn't similar to what we find in the "faith in Christ" texts. Paul does refer to Jesus's obedience in Romans 5:18–19 and Philippians 2:6–8, and those who support the "faithfulness of Christ" interpretation often appeal to these verses. But what stands out is that neither of these texts mention Jesus's "faithfulness." They use the words "obedience" and "obedient" instead, and so these two texts aren't very impressive evidence in favor of the subjective-genitive reading.

7. What stands out, if we consider the evidence, is that we have no clear evidence that Paul ever speaks of Christ's faithfulness in contexts relating to justification and salvation. On the other hand, Paul often speaks of faith in or believing in Jesus where salvation or justification is in view (Rom. 3:22; 10:9–14; Gal. 2:16; Eph. 1:15; Phil. 1:29; Col. 1:4; 2:5; Philem. 5). The way Paul speaks of faith and believing elsewhere naturally leads us to the conclusion that he has faith in Christ in mind.

8. Seeing a reference to faith in Christ makes more sense of the line of argument, the flow of thought, in Galatians 3:6–14. We read in 3:6 that Abraham was right with God because he "believed God." Paul doesn't speak of Abraham's faith in Christ here since Abraham lived before Jesus came to earth, but he pulls from the story of Abraham to emphasize that Abraham *believed God*. Galatians 3:7 draws a logical conclusion from Abraham's believing for the readers: "Know then that it is those of faith who are the sons of Abraham." The phrase "those of faith" must describe the faith the Galatians exercised since Paul draws a conclusion from Abraham's *believing* in 3:6. The same conclusion can be drawn from 3:8: "And the Scripture, foreseeing that God would justify the Gentiles by faith, preached the gospel beforehand to Abraham, saying, 'In you shall all the nations be blessed.'" Since

3:7 speaks of the faith of those who are part of Abraham's family, we rightly conclude that the same idea is in mind in 3:8. It would be very strange to read any idea of Christ's faithfulness into the text after the tight connection between believing and faith in 3:6–7. Just as Abraham was justified by believing, so those who are Abraham's children are also justified by their faith. Paul concludes the paragraph with the words, "So then, those who are of faith are blessed along with Abraham, the man of faith" (3:9). Once again the close logical relationship between 3:8 and 3:9 supports the idea that the faith of believers is in view. If it is the case in Galatians 3 that Paul refers to the faith of Abraham and the faith of believers, it is quite likely that the other references to faith (e.g., Gal. 2:16 and 2:20) should be understood as referring to the faith and trust of believers. After all, in both chapters the same subject—what is required for justification—is under consideration.

If we examine Galatians 3:10–14, we continue to see that a reference to faith in Christ is more likely. Paul begins by emphasizing that one must do everything the law requires to avoid the curse (3:10). He then contrasts justification through the law with the righteous who live by faith (3:11). It is quite doubtful that the reference here is to the faithfulness of Christ. Ordinary readers would naturally think that just as Abraham believed for justification so too believers must believe to be justified. We need to remember that there is no doubt that Abraham's faith is in view in 3:6 since Paul uses the verb "believed" with Abraham as the subject of the verb. This reading is confirmed even further in 3:12 where Paul says, "But the law is not of faith, rather 'The one who does them shall live by them.'" Paul contrasts and opposes two human activities—believing and doing. As noted before, we are right before God by believing not achieving, by trusting not performing, by resting in Christ not by meriting his grace. Paul concludes the paragraph with the following words: "so that we might receive the promised Spirit through faith" (3:14). The promise of the Spirit in 3:14 is parallel with the blessing of Abraham, and we saw earlier that Abraham was blessed because he believed, because of his faith. It seems quite clear, then, that the faith in view is the faith of human beings. They receive the blessing of Abraham because of their faith in Jesus.

After this fairly long discussion on faith in Jesus Christ, it is right to ask, Why is this important? Why should we even care? After all, both views make sense and fit within an orthodox framework. It matters because as readers of Scripture we want to know what Paul intends. We believe that the meaning of the scriptural text matters, and thus discerning what is intended is important. Furthermore, the role of faith in justification has been emphasized since the Reformation, and I believe with the Reformers that this emphasis is crucial. We are not justified or saved based on works but through faith in Jesus Christ. Faith is fundamentally receptive and thus communicates in a profound way our entire dependence on God in Christ for our justification. We don't rely on what we have done for our salvation but look away from ourselves to Jesus Christ. Our faith saves us because it looks to Christ and his death and resurrection for our righteousness. The message about faith in Christ is glorious because it lifts a burden that we could never fulfill. We rest in Christ for our justification instead of striving to attain it in our own strength.

We also see that faith *in Christ* is necessary for salvation. Paul doesn't merely call on us to believe to be justified. Our faith isn't vague and amorphous. Faith rests in, relies on, and trusts in Christ Jesus. Our faith is directed to a person, to Christ crucified and risen, to Jesus, who, as Paul says, "loved me and gave himself for me" (Gal. 2:20). As Paul says in Colossians, Christ is our life (Col. 3:4), and faith in Christ reminds us that we look to him for everything. He is our all in all. It makes sense, then, for Paul to say, "I live by faith in the Son of God" (Gal. 2:20). Faith isn't confined to the beginning of the Christian life but is what we are called to every day. The life of believers is one of trust. Believers received the Spirit because they heard the message of the gospel and believed (Gal. 3:2, 5), and they aren't perfected (3:3) in a different way. Trusting God for justification informs the whole of our lives as Christians.

The Basis of Justification

Justification means that people are declared to be in the right before God through faith in Jesus Christ, but the basis of this justification isn't faith itself. Faith is the means of justification but not its basis. The basis for God's declaration is the death and resurrection of Christ. The centrality of the cross was investigated in chapter 4, but here the role of the cross will be examined from a different angle so that we will probe more deeply how the cross and resurrection are the basis of justification.

Galatians 2:15–21 introduces the central theme of the letter. Even if one were to dissent from this claim, the text is very important, and it is the first time in the letter that Paul brings up the subject of justification. The words penned represent what Paul said to Peter after the latter's defection in Syrian Antioch, and though they are addressed to Peter they are meant for the Galatians. Paul affirms three times in 2:16 that justification is by faith in Jesus instead of by the works of the law. Since these words on justification represent Paul's response to Peter who was departing from "the truth of the gospel" (2:14), it follows that the truth of the gospel includes justification by faith. Then we see in 2:19–21 that justification by faith is rooted in Christ's death and resurrection. The Jewish teachers believed observing the law was the way to life, but Paul argues that believers must die to the law (2:19) and then rise to life again. This death and resurrection occurred when believers died with Christ and were raised with him (2:19–20). Righteousness is only ours through faith, for otherwise Christ died for nothing (2:21). Paul doesn't explain fully here the significance of the cross, but it is evident that faith is placed in Jesus as the crucified and risen Lord. Furthermore, his death is our death, and his life is our life.

A parallel text is Galatians 6:14 where Paul boasts only in the cross of Christ since by the cross "the world has been crucified to me, and I to the world." The expression isn't as explicit as we see in 2:19–20, but the same conception seems to be present. Life is ours only through death, and Jesus's death crucifies and puts to death the relation of believers to the world. Even though Paul doesn't unpack what he means in detail, it seems clear that the sin that dominates human beings is such that it is only broken through the death and resurrection of another—through the death and resurrection of Jesus Christ.

All students of Galatians recognize that 3:10–14 is one of the most important texts in the letter since Paul explains his understanding of justification in dialogue with Old Testament texts. We probably find in compact form arguments Paul used with both unbelieving Jews and Christians who were tempted to rely on the law for justification. Paul argues that perfect obedience to the law is needed to escape God's curse (3:10). Since no one keeps the law sufficiently to be justified, human beings are right before God by faith instead of through the observance of the law (3:11). The law and faith are diametrically opposed to one another since the former is based on doing and the latter on believing and receiving (3:12). But the key verse for our purposes is 3:13. The question that is raised is how the curse is removed from human beings since a curse extends to all those who fail to keep God's law. In other words, everyone is cursed because of disobedience. Freedom from the curse, redemption from the curse, is provided by Jesus Christ.

We noted earlier that redemption language is exodus language, and we recall how Israel was saved and redeemed from Egypt through the blood of the Passover lamb. In the new exodus, Israel will be redeemed "without money" (Isa. 52:3). Actually, Isaiah often speaks of Israel's new exodus in terms of redemption (Isa. 35:9; 41:14; 43:1, 14; 44:23, 24; 51:11; 62:12; 63:4, 9). Israel's redemption is described as the wiping away of her sins (Isa. 44:22). When we read the whole of Isaiah, however, the redemption in the new exodus occurs because of the servant of the Lord who took upon himself his people's sins. As Isaiah 53:5 says,

> He was pierced for our transgressions;
>   he was crushed for our iniquities;
>   upon him was the chastisement that brought us peace.

Israel would be redeemed through the atoning work of the Lord's servant, because

> the LORD has laid on him
> the iniquity of us all. (Isa. 53:6)

He was "stricken for the transgression of my people" (Isa. 53:8). His life was "an offering for guilt" (Isa. 53:10), and many will be counted as righteous since "he shall bear their iniquities" (Isa. 53:11) and "bore the sin of many" (Isa. 53:12). Israel was redeemed through the death of the servant, through his sacrifice as a guilt offering, as he took upon himself the sin of his people.

The redemption in Galatians 3:13 should be understood along the lines of the deliverance accomplished in the Passover and through the servant of the Lord. According to Paul the curse applies to all lawbreakers, and that means all without exception. Still, Christ freed his people by taking the curse upon himself "by becoming a curse for us" (3:13). The liberating and atoning work of the servant, the fulfillment of the new exodus, has become a reality through Jesus. He died in place of his people since he received the curse they deserved. Paul probably has the same conception in mind in 1:4, which we saw earlier also evokes the new exodus. The deliverance described is another way of talking about the freedom achieved in Jesus's death. Another way of putting it is that we are justified by faith because of the deliverance of Jesus, because he took upon himself the punishment we deserved.

The redeeming work of the cross is also featured in Galatians 4:4–5: "But when the fullness of time had come, God sent forth his Son, born of woman, born under the law, to redeem those who were under the law, so that we might receive adoption as sons." Once again we find that human beings need to be redeemed, liberated, and freed. Life under the law didn't translate into freedom and sonship but slavery (4:1, 3). Life as a slave fits with the need to be ransomed and freed. Liberation and adoption become a reality through the Son whom God sent to ransom those in bondage. The death of Christ, then, becomes the means by which the chains of sin that shackled human beings are shattered. My point is that our faith is directed to what Jesus accomplished in the cross. Faith saves, but it is a particular kind of faith—that is, faith in a particular object. Faith only saves because Christ saves by his work on the cross. Faith connects believers to the life-giving stream that is dispensed to us through Christ's self-giving and sacrificial work.

Conclusion

We have seen in this chapter that justification in Paul is forensic. Believers are declared to be right before God through faith in Christ. Salvation isn't obtained through keeping the law but by resting in and trusting in Christ. It is not as if our faith in itself saves. Faith saves because of the object of faith, because we put our faith in Jesus Christ as the crucified and risen Lord. Faith is an instrument of salvation, not its basis. Faith connects us to the one who truly saves.

6

The Law

Introduction

When we think of the theology in Galatians, we take one strand and examine it, but all themes naturally intersect and overlap so that we consider from a fresh angle matters that have been discussed under other headings. In this chapter, three topics will be investigated. First, Paul's rationale for saying that justification doesn't come via the law will be considered. Second, the law was not intended to rule over the people of God forever. The law is bound up with the covenant made with Israel at Mount Sinai, and that covenant has passed away. Third, we must then account for Paul's positive statements about the law, such as when he speaks of fulfilling the law (Gal. 5:14) and of fulfilling the law of Christ (6:2).

The Law Doesn't Justify

Paul declares three times in Galatians 2:16 that the works of the law don't justify, and then he reiterates this idea in 3:10. Twice he affirms that people don't receive the Spirit through the works of the law but only by faith (3:2, 5). There has been quite a tempest (though not in a teapot) over what "works of the law" means in Paul. Or, to put it another way, scholars disagree on why Paul rejects works of the law.[1]

---

1 I am going to concentrate on the most popular views instead of discussing all the views.

Some have suggested that works of the law are rejected because such works are legalistic.² Legalism should be defined as trying to earn favor with God by our obedience, by our good behavior. This interpretation isn't convincing. It reads "works of the law" as if Paul rejects them because of the *motive* or aim that animates our works. I am not saying that there is no polemic against legalism in Paul. But Paul says nothing about motives with reference to works of the law. Works of the law are ruled out for obtaining justification and receiving the Spirit *objectively*. In other words, even if our motives were perfectly good, we would still not be justified by the works of the law. Paul doesn't speak in terms of motives but in terms of facts. Justification cannot be gained via works of the law since, as we shall see, all fall short of what God requires.

A reading that has become quite popular in recent years is associated with the new perspective on Paul. This is not the place to dive into all the permutations and nuances of the new perspective. E. P. Sanders made it famous with his book *Paul and Palestinian Judaism*.³ Since Sanders's book was written in 1977, the new perspective isn't that new anymore! What Sanders argued is that Palestinian Judaism during the New Testament era was characterized by grace. Jews in the Second Temple period (ca. 400 BC to AD 200) didn't, according to Sanders, believe in works righteousness, nor were they legalistic. They didn't count up their works and base their salvation on the idea that they were 51 percent obedient. Instead, most Second Temple Jews were *covenant nomists* (from the Greek word *nomos*, meaning "law"). They believed that they entered into covenant with God by his grace and stayed in the covenant by works of the law. Their works, then, did not merit salvation. Instead Jews believed that they were saved by grace. Sanders's work is helpful in that it removed a caricature of Second Temple Jews, as if they

---

2   E.g., Ernest De Witt Burton, *A Critical and Exegetical Commentary on the Epistle to the Galatians*, ICC (New York: Scribner's, 1920), 120, 164; Ronald Y. K. Fung, *The Epistle to the Galatians*, NICNT (Grand Rapids, MI: Eerdmans, 1988), 113–14.

3   E. P. Sanders, *Paul and Palestinian Judaism: A Comparison of Patterns of Religions* (Philadelphia: Fortress, 1977).

were consumed with legalistic self-righteousness. Still, Sanders's own reading of Judaism is overly simplistic, and his attempt to wash out all legalism or works righteousness from Second Temple Judaism doesn't entirely succeed. We see this in the many books that have qualified or contested Sanders's reading.[4] Sanders's paradigm needs to be adjusted since recent scholarship has shown that his reading of the sources is too one-dimensional. A focus on obedience and even works righteousness is present in some of the sources.

The issue before us, however, is the understanding of works of the law according to Paul. James Dunn and N. T. Wright have led the way in proposing a new way of conceiving the works of the law.[5] Both Dunn and Wright accept Sanders's reading of Second Temple Judaism. If Sanders is on target and the problem with the law can't be traced to works righteousness and legalism, then why did Paul reject the law as a way of salvation? According to Dunn and Wright, the traditional understanding of the law and justification that has been advanced among Protestants since the Reformation can't be accepted since that reading was built on a shaky foundation, on the claim that the Jews of the first century were guilty of works righteousness and legalism like the Roman Catholics of the sixteenth century. But if the traditional Protestant reading goes astray, then why does Paul say that works of the law don't justify? Dunn and Wright propose that works of the law

---

4 See, e.g., Mark A. Elliott, *The Survivors of Israel: A Reconsideration of the Theology of Pre-Christian Judaism* (Grand Rapids, MI: Eerdmans, 2000); D. A. Carson, Peter T. O'Brien, and Mark A. Seifrid, eds., *The Complexities of Second Temple Judaism*, vol. 1 of *Justification and Variegated Nomism* (Grand Rapids, MI: Baker, 2001); Simon Gathercole, *Where Is Boasting? Early Jewish Soteriology and Paul's Response in Romans 1–5* (Grand Rapids, MI: Eerdmans, 2003). For some problems with such a reading of Paul, see also John M. G. Barclay, *Paul and the Gift* (Grand Rapids, MI: Eerdmans, 2015). See my appendix for a summary and evaluation of this important book by Barclay.

5 James D. G. Dunn, "Works of the Law and the Curse of the Law (Galatians 3.10–14)," *NTS* 31 (1985): 523–42; "Yet Once More—'the Works of the Law': A Response," *JSNT* 46 (1992): 99–117. Dunn has adjusted his interpretation to some extent. See J. D. G. Dunn "What's Right about the Old Perspective?," in *Studies in the Pauline Epistles: Essays in Honor of Douglas J. Moo*, ed. M. Harmon and J. E. Smith (Grand Rapids, MI: Zondervan, 2014), 214–29. But Wright seems more settled on the matter. N. T. Wright, "Paul and the Patriarch: The Role of Abraham in Romans 4," *JSNT* 35 (2013): 207–41.

focus on the Jewish boundary markers, the badges that separate Jews from Gentiles. The boundary markers consisted of those things that segregate Jews from Gentiles, such as Sabbath, circumcision, and food laws. When we read authors from the Greco-Roman world, we find that they were puzzled and often offended that Jews would not work on Saturday, that they would not eat with Gentiles because of their purity laws, and that they separated themselves from others because of the covenant mark of circumcision.

Support for the notion that works of the law center on boundary markers is found in the controversy that took place in Antioch over Peter and other Jewish Christians eating with Gentiles (Gal. 2:11–14). When James raised concerns about the purity laws being violated, Peter and his Jewish colleagues quit eating with the Gentiles. Supporters of the new perspective argue that Galatians 2:11–14 indicates that the debate in Galatia was over laws that segregated Jews from Gentiles. The new perspective rightly sees that boundary markers were an issue in the early church, and we must not overreact to the new perspective since it rightly emphasizes a major theme in Paul's theology. The cultural and ethnic differences between Jews and Gentiles in the first century were significant, and Paul emphasizes that the wall dividing Jews from Gentiles has come down (Eph. 2:11–22). Now Jews and Gentiles who trust in Jesus belong equally to the people of God. It would be a mistake, then, to reject every insight of the new perspective. The conflict culturally between Jews and Gentiles was significant in the first century and in Paul's thought, showing up in the controversy over circumcision, purity laws, and the Sabbath. Nevertheless, despite this valid insight in the new perspective, ethnocentrism and the boundary markers are not Paul's primary critique against the Jews of his day. Instead, he argues that works of the law do not justify since all sin and violate the torah.

Here we need to remind ourselves of what Paul says about the law. The phrase "works of the law" is found six times in Galatians. We are informed three times in Galatians 2:16 that justification doesn't come via works of the law. In 3:2 and 3:5 Paul emphasizes that one does not receive the Spirit by works of the law, while in 3:10 he declares that works of the law lead to a curse. Similarly, 2:21 affirms that righteousness is not attained or obtained through the law. In 3:11 Paul affirms that it is obvious and clear that no one is justified by the law, while in 5:4 we discover that those who are attempting to be justified by the law have fallen from grace. The opposition between law and grace in the letter is pervasive and illuminating. Since the law enjoins obedience, it isn't a distortion of what Paul writes to see an emphasis on doing, on human performance, on obedience. Grace, on the other hand, emphasizes God's work, his supernatural power, and the gift granted to human beings. We see this theme as well in Romans 11:6, where Paul tells us that grace and works are fundamentally opposed. I suggest that the new perspective is flawed not in what it affirms but in what it denies. Yes, ethnocentrism was a problem among Jews in the first century, but it was not the fundamental problem. The fundamental problem with the Jews and with all of us—the worm in the apple, so to speak—is the sin that indwells human beings. God judges human beings, both Jews and Gentiles, because they fail to do his will.

When we examine the issue further, we have additional evidence that works of the law are rejected because of human sin. Galatians 3:10 is crucial and fundamental:[6] "For all who rely on works of the law are under a curse; for it is written, 'Cursed be everyone who does not abide by all things written in the Book of the Law, and do them.'" Paul explains why those who are of the works of the law are under a curse. He quotes Deuteronomy 27:26, which pronounces a curse on those who do not keep the law. If we examine Galatians 3:10 closely, we find that perfect obedience to the law is required. Notice that the curse falls on those who do not keep "*all* things written in the Book of the Law." This fits with Deuteronomy 28:58, which Paul also likely alludes to, where Moses says the people must be "careful to do all the words of this law that are written in this book." Interestingly, Paul doesn't say that no one

---

6   Thomas R. Schreiner, "Paul and Perfect Obedience to the Law: An Evaluation of the View of E. P. Sanders," *WTJ* 47 (1985): 245–78; Thomas R. Schreiner, "Is Perfect Obedience to the Law Possible? A Re-examination of Galatians 3:10," *JETS* 27 (1984): 151–60.

can keep the law. But the reason for this isn't hard to find. There was no need to specify that all fall short of what God commands because this is taught often in the Old Testament (e.g., 1 Kings 8:46; Prov. 20:9; Eccl. 7:20), and we also see sin in the lives of the best Old Testament characters—such as Abraham, Moses, David, and others. I conclude that works of the law do not justify since God demands perfect obedience, and no one carries out all that God requires.

Some object to this interpretation. They point out that the Old Testament didn't demand perfect obedience. When Israel sinned, atonement was provided through animal sacrifices, and thus perfect obedience wasn't necessary. The question is pertinent, helping us to gain a clearer perspective on what Paul is teaching. It is true that in the Old Testament those who sinned were granted forgiveness by God's mercy through sacrifices. What this observation misses, however, is that a new covenant has arrived in Jesus Christ. The Old Testament sacrifices were a *temporary* provision until the coming of the Messiah. Now that the Christ has come, the curse from the law is only removed through his atoning sacrifice. Galatians 3:13 clearly teaches us this: "Christ redeemed us from the curse of the law by becoming a curse for us—for it is written, 'Cursed is everyone who is hanged on a tree.'" We see the same truth in Galatians 2:21 where Paul declares that if right standing with God comes via the law, then Christ died for nothing.

It is true, then, that in one sense perfect obedience wasn't required under the old covenant since animal sacrifices could be offered to receive forgiveness. On the other hand, the very fact that there were such sacrifices indicates that every sin must either be punished or atoned for. To put it another way, the need for sacrifices for sin shows that perfection was required. Israel needed to be forgiven for its sin. It is imperative to recognize that Paul's point is also salvation historical. The old covenant with its sacrifices has passed away since, as will be argued further below, the covenant with Israel is now obsolete. Thus, those who rely on the law for salvation must keep the law perfectly since the atonement provided by Old Testament sacrifices is no longer effective now that Christ has come. If one relies on the law for salvation, including the animal sacrifices offered for forgiveness and cleansing, then one is cutting oneself off from the death of Christ. Since animal sacrifices no longer atone, those who put themselves under the law must keep the law flawlessly. Since such perfect obedience is impossible, a curse rests on those who rely on the works of the law. How does this discussion of works of the law relate to the new perspective? We see from Galatians 3:10 that "works of the law" refers to the entire law. Furthermore, the fundamental reason for the curse is neither ethnocentrism nor boundary markers. Rather, the curse lies on those who do not keep God's law.

What Galatians says about works of the law fits with the letter to the Romans. In Romans 3:20 and 28 Paul teaches that justification isn't obtained through works of the law. When we look at the argument of Romans 1:18–3:20, which explains why human beings aren't righteous through the works of the law, Paul does not concentrate on the boundary markers. The indictment of the Jews in Romans 2 focuses on their disobedience, on their failure to keep the law. For instance, in Romans 2:1–3 the Jews are criticized for doing the same things, committing the same sins, as the Gentiles. This fits with Romans 2:5–11 where judgment is according to works. Similarly, Paul stresses that the Jews will be assessed by whether they observe the law, and thus "all who have sinned under the law will be judged by the law. For it is not the hearers of the law who are righteous before God, but the doers of the law who will be justified" (Rom. 2:12–13). It is interesting that Paul says nothing about excluding Gentiles or about boundary markers when he indicts the Jews. Instead he concentrates on Jewish lawlessness. This fits with Romans 2:17–24 where Paul recounts various Jewish advantages, especially stressing the gift of the law and the privilege the Jews have of teaching others about the content of the law.

Some commentators make the mistake of thinking that Paul criticizes the Jews for their special relation to God, but such a judgment goes astray. The fault of the Jews is not that they have special salvation-historical advantages, for such privileges were given to them by God himself! No, the complaint is that they don't keep the very law they treasure and teach. They teach that one must not steal, but they themselves steal. They admonish people not to commit adultery, but they commit adultery. They are repulsed by idols, but they rob idols' temples. What is especially interesting is that the sins listed all represent moral infractions of the law; nothing is said about boundary markers. Paul does mention circumcision (Rom. 2:25–29), but again he doesn't complain that they exclude Gentiles but that they don't keep the law.

Finally, Romans 3:9–18 drive us to the same conclusion. Paul tells us that no one is righteous, no one seeks God, no one does what is good. All fall short in their speech, which is deceptive and poisonous and harmful. Also, they violate God's will in that they shed the blood of others and inflict misery and injury on others. Once again, the focus is on the moral blemishes that characterize all human beings, both Jews and Gentiles. Romans, then, leads us to the same conclusion regarding works of the law that we found in Galatians. Works of the law do not and cannot justify since God demands perfection and all fall short of what he requires. I conclude, then, that the works of the law embrace everything commanded in the torah. Actually, the new perspective has it backwards since when Paul indicts the Jewish people he doesn't focus on the boundary markers but the moral law. The curse comes on all people via the law since all without exception transgress what God commands.

The problem with the law is that it doesn't curb sin but exacerbates it, and a number of texts in Galatians confirm this judgment. For instance, we read in Galatians 3:19, "Why then the law? It was added because of transgressions, until the offspring should come to whom the promise had been made, and it was put in place through angels by an intermediary." This verse is interpreted in various ways.[7] Some think that Paul suggests that the law was introduced to curb and limit human sin. Others defend the notion that the law was introduced to define human sin. The context in Galatians, however, supports the

---

[7] For further discussion, see Thomas R. Schreiner, *Galatians*, ZECNT (Grand Rapids, MI: Zondervan, 2010), 239–40.

idea that sin increases with the advent of the law. Galatians 3:21–23 supports this conclusion:

> If a law had been given that could give life, then righteousness would indeed be by the law. But the Scripture imprisoned everything under sin, so that the promise by faith in Jesus Christ might be given to those who believe. Now before faith came, we were held captive under the law, imprisoned until the coming faith would be revealed.

We discover a few things about the law here. First, the law could not grant life to human beings. In other words, there is no power in the law that transforms human beings so that they are enabled to do what pleases God. Or, as the second part of the verse says, the law doesn't make people righteous. It seems, then, that the law reveals the fallenness of human beings. This fits, secondly, with the next thing Paul says—namely, that everything is imprisoned under sin. He makes this observation in a context discussing the law, confirming that the law isn't the agent God uses to change human hearts. Third, Paul speaks of the law in terms of captivity and imprisonment. This should not be interpreted as if the law restrains or limits sin. Instead the law becomes a means by which human beings are enslaved. The law doesn't give life but shines a light on the fleshiness of human beings, showing that we need redemption through Jesus Christ. This reading of Galatians is strengthened by consulting Romans. There Paul says that the law was introduced so that sin might increase (Rom. 5:20). Obviously, there are differences between Romans and Galatians, but we expect Paul's theology of the law to agree in the two letters, even if there are different emphases.

The problem with the law, then, is not the content of the law but the inherent capacity and nature of human beings. The law brings a curse and judgment since those who are under the law are under the authority and power of sin. We see this clearly in Gal. 5:18: "But if you are led by the Spirit, you are not under the law." This is quite a remarkable statement. Those who are directed by the Spirit are not under the law, whereas by way of contrast those who are under the law are also under the power of sin. We see in this text that Paul ties together the law and sin, not because the law is sinful but because the law doesn't produce the transformation needed for human flourishing.

The inadequacy of the law also shows up in Galatians 4:3, where Paul speaks of being enslaved under the elements of the world. What Paul means by the word "elements" (*stoicheia*) is debated intensely.[8] But we don't need to resolve that question for our purposes. It seems fair to say, however, that Paul is merging together the notion of being under the elements with being under the law. Amazingly, Paul connects the desire of the Galatians to observe the law to turning back to the elements that are "weak and worthless" (4:9). The Galatians as Gentiles weren't turning back to life under torah, for they weren't under the Jewish torah before they were converted to Christ. They lived as pagans, enslaved to false gods. We could easily miss, then, how shocking the reference to elements is since Paul compares the Galatians' desire to be under the law to returning to paganism! Since being under the elements is equivalent to being under the law, it is clear that life under the law enslaves instead of liberates. Life under the law doesn't tamp down sin but enflames and activates sin.

The theme of slavery also appears in Paul's allegory of the two women (Gal. 4:21–5:1). The children of Hagar, whom Paul aligns with those who are under the law and with the covenant made at Mount Sinai, are enslaved. The *slave* Hagar represents those under the Sinai covenant. The connection of Hagar with Mount Sinai and the law is a bold move, one that would astonish those who saw the law as the path to virtue. Paul contrasts the heavenly Jerusalem with the earthly city. The former is the mother of those who are free, and the free children are like Isaac instead of the slave Ishmael. Paul could scarcely be clearer: the law doesn't emancipate but incarcerates people. Finally, we see the incapacity of the law even in the lives of those who promoted the law

---

8   For further discussion, see Schreiner, *Galatians*, 267–69.

for salvation. Paul remarks, "For even those who are circumcised do not themselves keep the law, but they desire to have you circumcised that they may boast in your flesh" (Gal. 6:13). Paul's adversaries do not keep the law themselves. Rather, the law is turned into a means for self-exaltation.

I conclude this section with the observation that the law does not save or justify, not because the law is inferior in any way. The problem lies in human beings, in sin, in disobedience, in rebellion. Paul's fundamental critique against the law, then, isn't that the law divides Jews from Gentiles, even though there is some truth in that claim. Still, the root problem is human sin, so that the reason the law does not save is because of human fallibility.

Temporary Nature of the Covenant with Israel

Paul's argument against circumcision isn't only anthropological, which means that he doesn't restrict himself to human sin and human inability and human incapacity. Circumcision is also set aside for salvation-historical reasons. We could imagine Paul saying that circumcision isn't required for salvation, just as many today would say that baptism isn't required for salvation, and yet they might go on to argue that a person should be baptized because it is one of God's commandments. Paul, however, does not follow this approach. He doesn't say that even though circumcision isn't mandated for salvation, it should be observed by faith as one of God's commandments. Instead, he argues that circumcision isn't required at all, that the command is no longer in force. Paul's argument is covenantal and redemptive historical. Circumcision isn't required now that the old covenant has passed away.

We see the temporary character of the covenant mediated by Moses in Galatians 3:15–18. A covenant, once it is ratified, cannot be set aside, nor can further provisions be added to it. Paul applies this to the covenants made with Abraham and with Israel at Mount Sinai. In doing so he distinguishes the two covenants. This may not seem significant, but the radical nature of Paul's gospel again surfaces since the Jews of Paul's day would have equated the two covenants, or perhaps better they would not have seen any discontinuity between them. Some Jewish writers even argued that Abraham kept the stipulations of the covenant made with Israel (cf. Gen. 26:5). Paul notes, however, that the covenant with Israel originated 430 years after the covenant made with Abraham. This later covenant, Paul remarks, cannot invalidate the promises given to Abraham and his offspring. In this sense, the covenant with Abraham has a different character and nature than the covenant mediated by Moses. The covenant with Abraham contains promises that cannot be invalidated. On the other hand, the covenant with Moses stands in contrast with the promises made to Abraham. In other words, its fulfillment depends on human obedience instead of the divine promise. The surety of God's promises in the covenant with Abraham is guaranteed since his offspring is Christ (Gal. 3:16), but the covenant with Israel ratified on Mount Sinai isn't based solely on God's gracious promise but also on the obedience of human beings. The temporal interval between the two covenants and their different natures signal that the covenant at Sinai is temporary. It is an intermediary covenant that was established 430 years after the covenant with Abraham, but now that Christ has come the intermediary covenant has come to an end.

The provisional nature of the covenant at Sinai is supported by Galatians 3:19. This verse teaches that the law was added to promote human sin, as I argued earlier. But we should note that the law, according to this verse, is in place "until the offspring should come." We saw above that the offspring promised to Abraham is Christ himself (Gal. 3:16), and now with the coming of Christ the law, the covenant made with Israel, has passed away. The law points to and finds its fulfillment and end in Christ himself (cf. Rom. 10:4). We find a similar conception in Galatians 3:23–25 where Paul refers to the time before the coming of faith. The faith in view here is specifically faith in Christ. The law is described as our *paidagōgos*, which is translated in a number of different ways: "guardian" (ESV, CSB, NIV, NET), "schoolmaster" (KJV), "custodian" (RSV), "tutor" (NASB

1995). The word doesn't refer to a teacher, tutor, or instructor but to one who attends to and cares for a child during growing-up years.[9] I think the word "babysitter" is the best dynamic translation of the term. Babysitters are appropriate while we are growing up, but they are dispensed with at adulthood. Paul applies this notion to the law, so that we read in Galatians 3:24 that we need a guardian or a babysitter only *until* Christ comes. Now that Christ has come, our time under a babysitter has ended. This is confirmed in Galatians 3:25: the coming of Christ means that we are *no longer* under a guardian. In other words, the old covenant, the covenant made with Israel at the time of Moses, the covenant that requires circumcision, has passed away.[10]

Another text that teaches the temporary function of the law is Galatians 4:1–7. Paul compares believers to children who are still under guardians and managers. In that sense they are comparable to slaves. Incidentally, the word "slave" (4:1) reveals Paul's understanding of the law. Being a child under guardians, after all, isn't necessarily equivalent to slavery, but Paul crafts the illustration a particular way to emphasize the nature of life under the law. Thus, he proceeds to say that unbelievers were enslaved under the elements of the world. But now a new era of redemptive history has dawned with the coming of Jesus Christ so that believers are no longer slaves but sons. Life under the law is like being under guardians and managers and lasts during infancy, but the days of infancy have come to an end with the coming of Jesus Christ. The role of the law as guardian and manager no longer applies.

Paul's use of the "under" (*hypo*) phrases also demonstrates that a new era of salvation history has arrived and that believers are not under the administration of the Sinai covenant. This discussion overlaps some with what was previously discussed, but the overlap is

---

9 See Schreiner, *Galatians*, 248–49.
10 Given what Paul says earlier about the law promoting sin, the reference to the law as guardian doesn't teach that the law curbs sin (like a babysitter restrains evil in children). The point of the illustration is the *temporary* need for a guardian.

worth pointing out, since it underscores and confirms what has been said earlier about the law.

- Those who attach themselves to works of the law are "under a curse" (Gal. 3:10).
- Scripture has enclosed all "under sin" (3:22).
- Before faith in Christ came, people were held in custody "under the law" (3:23).
- Believers are freed from being "under a guardian" (3:25).
- Minors are "under guardians and managers" until the time of maturity (4:2).
- Unbelievers are enslaved "under [ESV: "to"] the elementary principles of the world" (4:3).
- Jesus was also born "under the law" (4:4).
- Jesus liberates those "under the law" (4:5).
- The Galatians apparently desired to be "under the law" (4:21).
- Those who are directed by the Spirit are not "under the law" (5:18).

For the sake of completeness we could add Romans 6:14–15, which affirms that believers aren't "under law" but "under grace." We see from these parallel phrases that life under the law represents a time in history that has passed away. This is clear from Galatians 4:4–5 in that Jesus was born under the law, but he was born under the law in order to free and redeem those under the law. Now that the new era in redemptive history has arrived through the work of Jesus Christ and the gift of the Holy Spirit, the time of the law has come to an end.

What this means for circumcision is clear. Circumcision has ended along with the old covenant, the old era, the previous time in salvation history. To insist on circumcision for salvation, then, is to turn the clock back in redemptive history. Requiring circumcision acts as if Jesus Christ had not come and as if the Holy Spirit had not been given. The requirement of circumcision is like living under the moonlight after the day has dawned, when the sun is shining in all its brilliant fullness.

Fulfilling the Law

Paul emphasizes that believers are not under the law, that the law belongs to a previous era of redemptive history. So it is quite surprising to find him saying that believers fulfill the whole law. We read in Galatians 5:14, "For the whole law is fulfilled in one word: 'You shall love your neighbor as yourself.'" The provocative nature of such an admonition stands out even further when we consider 5:3: "I testify again to every man who accepts circumcision that he is obligated to keep the whole law." In 5:3 Paul rejects the notion that believers should put themselves under the whole law, reminding them that they would take upon themselves an onerous and impossible burden. But then in 5:14 he speaks positively of fulfilling the whole law. Some have maintained that Paul is contradictory, but that should be rejected categorically. After all, these statements are only ten verses apart. It is difficult to believe that Paul himself did not notice the tension present in these two different affirmations. Since Paul put them so close together, he expected his readers to reflect on what he meant at a deeper level. Of course, the tension isn't only between two verses but also relates to what is taught about the law in the letter as a whole.

In Greek the words "the whole law" are different in Galatians 5:3 (*holon ton nomon*) and 5:14 (*ho pas nomos*), but we should not make too much of that difference. Paul isn't thinking of the whole law in a different sense in 5:3 and 5:14. It is more promising to observe the different verbs that are used relative to the law in these two verses. We notice in 5:3 that Paul uses the verb "keep" or "do" (*poiēsai*), while in 5:14 the verb is "fulfill" (*peplērōtai*). Paul's use of the word "fulfill" is instructive in this regard. For example, in Romans 8:4 he says that those who have the Spirit fulfill the law, and this fits with the context of Galatians 5–6 where believers live in a transformed way by the power of the Spirit. Perhaps an even more striking parallel surfaces in Romans 13:8–10. Here we are told that those who love their neighbors fulfill the law. Paul proceeds after this to cite various commands from the decalogue, such as don't commit adultery, don't murder, don't steal, and don't covet. All these commands fill in and explain the command to love our neighbors as ourselves, and Paul then concludes, "Love is the fulfilling of the law" (Rom. 13:10). Paul, therefore, doesn't talk about *doing* the law or *obeying* the law in Galatians in a positive sense but *fulfilling* the law. The word "fulfill" has an eschatological sense, showing that the law is fulfilled as God's redemptive promises are realized in Jesus Christ. The eschatological dimension of fulfilling the law also appears in a context where the power of the Holy Spirit is emphasized in Galatians, and the Spirit is the gift of the new age, the new covenant. The reference to the Spirit underscores that the law isn't fulfilled autonomously but supernaturally, with divine power.

Another observation pertaining to the fulfillment of the law should be mentioned. According to both Galatians and Romans, we fulfill the law through love.[11] The commandments play a role because commands describe what love looks like in everyday life. Nevertheless, the commands of the law are not central in Paul's ethic; *love* is central. Love is the heart and soul of Paul's ethic. On the other hand, love without commands is plastic so that it is in danger of being defined according to the whims and inclinations of human beings. The commands, then, show us what love is like in action. They save us from sentimentality where love dissolves into mere feelings of affection. Love is concrete, realistic, and manifests itself in particular ways. Still, love goes far beyond commands. We can imagine someone who refrains from adultery, murder, and stealing while being self-absorbed, narcissistic, and irritable. Love never transgresses commands, which is to say that love never violates moral norms. Nevertheless, love is not fully encapsulated or defined by such moral norms. Love is more than keeping moral norms but is never less than that.

It is here that we should consider Paul's words, "against such things there is no law" (Gal. 5:23). He says this after listing the fruit of the Spirit. His point seems to be that the law doesn't produce the kind

---

11   For the theology of law in Paul, see Brian S. Rosner, *Paul and the Law: Keeping the Commandments of God*, NSBT 31 (Downers Grove, IL: InterVarsity Press, 2013); Thomas R. Schreiner, *The Law and Its Fulfillment: A Pauline Theology of Law* (Grand Rapids, MI: Baker Books, 1993); Thomas R. Schreiner, *40 Questions About Christians and Biblical Law* (Grand Rapids, MI: Kregel, 2010).

of life that pleases God. The commands of the law, as we saw above, may express what love looks like in everyday life. But those who live by the power of the Spirit live out a life of love regardless of what the law says. This is just another way of saying that the law isn't the means of life. The Jews often connected the law with life, and in this respect Paul departs from a common Jewish perspective, one that he almost certainly shared before he became a Christian.

We still need to answer the question, however, of how Paul can speak of Christians fulfilling the law when the covenant made with Israel at Mount Sinai has passed away. One reason this is difficult is because Paul doesn't answer this question directly. How can Paul say that believers are no longer under the law and then turn around and say that believers fulfill the law? To put it another way, how can Paul cite certain commands from the law as authoritative if believers are no longer under the law? If the covenant with Israel has passed away, then believers are no longer under the stipulations of that covenant. The commands Paul quotes are not authoritative because they come from the Mosaic law; they are authoritative because they represent the will of God. As Brian Rosner says, they describe wisdom, a way of life that pleases God and leads to human flourishing.[12] Another way of putting it is this: the commands are in force because they describe God's character and being. So we have to distinguish between the covenant made with Israel and norms within that covenant that are transcendent and morally applicable in every era. The Pauline writings and the entire New Testament assist us so that we are able to discern what commands in the covenant made with Israel continue to be applicable today. We could summarize by saying that the commands that are universal, those that are moral norms, are the will of God for believers today. If we probe deeper, we find that they are moral norms because they represent God's character.

We also find the notion of fulfillment in Galatians 6:2. The CSB catches the sense: "Carry one another's burdens; in this way you will

---

[12] Rosner, *Paul and the Law*, 159–205.

fulfill the law of Christ." We don't have the exact same verb as "fulfill" (*plēroō*) in 5:14, but there is a clear play on words in 6:2 where the word "fulfill" has the Greek prepositional prefix *ana-* (*anaplēroō*). Thus, there is no significant change in meaning. Scholars dispute what Paul means by "the of law of Christ" in 6:2, but it seems clear that Paul enunciates a new law, which is no longer the law of Moses but the law of Christ. Believers are no longer under the covenant made with Israel and the provisions of that covenant. Believers live under a new covenant where Christ is King, and thus they live according to his law.

When we look at Galatians 6:2 and 5:14, we can see a relationship between these two verses. Both speak of fulfilling the law, but in 6:2 the law is described as "the law of Christ." To carry the burdens of others is to love others, and we saw in 5:14 that the whole law is fulfilled in love. So, given the connections between the two verses, it seems fair to say that the law of Christ is the law of love. Why is it called the law of Christ? I have already said that we're under a new covenant where Christ is our King, and in that sense he gives us commands. But we can also say that it is identified as the law of Christ because Christ exemplifies what the law of love looks like.[13] Christ functions as a paradigm of love in his self-giving for others, particularly in suffering death for the sake of his people. Christ lived an other-directed life, one where he met the needs of others, and thus he is an example to us—the greatest example—of what love looks like in everyday life.

The law of Christ should not be viewed as an onerous burden, as if it consisted of many detailed regulations. The law of Christ is not a new Mishnah but a way of living in the world, a way of life that manifests the love of Christ. In other words, those who fulfill the law of Christ do so out of their love for Christ, and we must not forget that believers are empowered by the Holy Spirit. The paradox of living under the law of Christ is evident in 1 Corinthians 9:21: "To those outside the law I became as one outside the law (not being outside the law of God but under the law of Christ) that I might win those outside the law." In one

---

13 See Richard B. Hays, "Christology and Ethics in Galatians: The Law of Christ," *CBQ* 49 (1987): 268–90.

sense, Paul is no longer under the law since the Mosaic covenant and its stipulations are no longer in force for believers. Thus, Paul can declare that he is free from the law. On the other hand, he doesn't want to convey the sense that he stands outside of moral norms, and thus he abides by the law of Christ. Still, this law gives him cultural flexibility so that he can reach all people with the gospel. This means that sometimes Paul keeps the stipulations found in the old covenant, and sometimes he lives in freedom and does not adhere to these rules. The rules he doesn't keep are almost certainly the commands separating Jews from Gentiles, such as purity laws. Still, Paul's flexibility to such requirements doesn't mean that he leads a lawless life. Paul exemplifies the law of Christ in that in every situation he lives in a way that is loving, whether he is with Jews or Gentiles. Love, in this instance, shows itself in the desire to win all to Christ, to save if at all possible all kinds of people.

Conclusion

We have seen in this chapter three truths. First, the law does not and cannot save since God demands perfect obedience and human beings fail to carry out the requirements of the law. The problem, then, is not with the law but with human sin. The new perspective rightly sees that the division between Jews and Gentiles was a major issue in Paul's ministry and theology. Still, the new perspective falls short in that it fails to see that Paul's fundamental complaint with reference to the law is that human beings fail to keep it. Second, the law—that is, the stipulations given to Israel on Mount Sinai—is no longer in force. Believers are no longer under the covenant made with Moses and Israel. The old covenant was always intended to be temporary and provisional, and the covenant with Abraham is the fundamental covenant. Third, believers are free from the law of Moses, but they live by the law of Christ, which is nothing other than the law of love. This pattern of love is exemplified in Christ himself. Saying that the law of Christ is the law of love doesn't lead to the conclusion that there are no moral norms. Moral norms are still in force because they represent God's very character, and in that sense they are transcendent norms that do not pass away.

PART 3
―――――

THE NEW LIFE

7

The Family of Abraham

Introduction

Paul in the letter to the Galatians doesn't articulate his understanding of the church in the same way that we see, for example, in the epistle to the Ephesians. Nevertheless, we do glean from the letter an understanding of the people of God. And the banner we could drape over this understanding is that the people of God are understood to be the family of Abraham. I should note at this point that the new perspective rightly emphasizes this theme in Paul's letters. The unity of the people of God is prized by Paul. The cultural barriers that segregated Jews from Gentiles have now come down in Jesus Christ.

For the Jews in the Old Testament and the Second Temple period, one became a member of God's people through circumcision (Gen. 17:9–14). If one belonged to the people of God, one was a child of Abraham. If one wasn't a child of Abraham, one wasn't a child of God. Paul as a Jew nurtured in the Old Testament agreed that one must belong to Abraham's family to be a member of God's people. In this way he was a fully orthodox Jew. What set him apart, however, was his conviction that in Christ Jesus one became a child of Abraham through faith, and circumcision was not required. We see this clearly in Galatians 3:7–9:

> Know then that it is those of faith who are the sons of Abraham. And the Scripture, foreseeing that God would justify the Gentiles by faith,

preached the gospel beforehand to Abraham, saying, "In you shall all the nations be blessed." So then, those who are of faith are blessed along with Abraham, the man of faith.

Paul redraws Abraham's family around the faith of Abraham instead of the circumcision of Abraham, and such a redrawing was a radical redefinition of the people of God. Gentiles could now be counted as members of the people of God, members of the family of Abraham if they had the faith of Abraham. Thus, Jews who do not have the faith of Abraham are actually like Ishmael in Paul's famous allegory (Gal. 4:21–31). Conversely, those who have faith like Abraham are actually like Isaac, the true child of Abraham, even if they are not circumcised and do not observe the law.

Paul reconceives the family of God in Christological terms. The most stunning example of this appears in Galatians 3:16, for Christ is said to be the one true offspring of Abraham. But if Christ is the offspring of Abraham, then the fundamental question is whether one belongs to Jesus Christ. The people of God are not shaped by their observance of the law but by their faith in Christ. We see this clearly in 3:29: "And if you are Christ's, then you are Abraham's offspring, heirs according to promise." Membership in Abraham's family is reserved for those who are joined with Jesus by faith. We understand, then, why Paul affirms that "in Christ Jesus you are all sons of God" (3:26). We must not miss the word "all," for "all" includes both Jews and Gentiles as God's sons. Still, being a son or daughter of God only occurs in Christ Jesus. Paul underscores the truth of the gospel, which is that the people of God are painted in Christological colors.

The People of God

The Israel of God

Two very interesting implications follow from Paul's understanding of the people of God. We consider first Galatians 6:16: "And as for all who walk by this rule, peace and mercy be upon them, and upon the Israel of God."[1] The meaning of "the Israel of God" is intensely debated. Does Paul include Gentile Christians in the Israel of God or is the expression limited to Jewish Christians? Greek grammar plays a role so that scholars debate whether the Greek word *kai* means "and" or "even." The use of the word "and" doesn't necessarily mean that the reference is to Jewish Christians, but the conjunction could be interpreted in this way. The NIV clearly understands the word *kai* as identifying both Jews and Gentiles as members of the Israel of God: "Peace and mercy to all who follow this rule—to the Israel of God." In my judgment the NIV translation represents Paul's meaning so that Gentiles are included in the Israel of God.

The meaning of the phrase can't be established or proven on the basis of grammatical arguments since different understandings of the grammar can be supported. Instead, we need to look at the message of the entire letter to discern what Paul means by "the Israel of God." When we consider the argument that is made in the entire letter, it is difficult to believe in this context that "the Israel of God" could mean anything other than the church of Jesus Christ composed of both Jews and Gentiles. After all, the issue in Galatians hangs on who are the true people of God and what marks out someone as a member of the true people of God. Paul has argued clearly in Galatians 3–4 that Gentiles who put their faith in Jesus Christ are the true children of Abraham. Now at the end of the letter (Gal. 6:11–18) his purpose is to sum up some of the major themes of the letter. It would be highly confusing if in his closing words Paul limited the Israel of God to Jewish Christians. Such a conclusion would be the view of the Jewish teachers who are criticized so fiercely throughout the letter. Paul declares in a final climactic and definitive statement that those who belong to Jesus Christ constitute God's Israel.

This is not to say that whenever Paul uses the term "Israel" in his letters that it invariably refers to the church of Jesus Christ. Context

---

1 For a fuller discussion of this verse, see Thomas R. Schreiner, *Galatians*, ZECNT (Grand Rapids, MI: Zondervan, 2010), 381–83.

is decisive in determining what Paul means by "Israel." For instance, it seems clear in Romans 9–11 that the term "Israel" is reserved exclusively or at least mainly for Jews or Jewish Christians. We need to recognize that the context in Galatians is dramatically different, and that Paul at the end of the letter would send a most confusing signal if he suddenly inserted the idea that God's Israel consists of Jewish Christians, when he has argued throughout that Gentile believers are members of Abraham's family. This understanding of the Israel of God fits naturally with what was pointed out earlier that the people of God are Christologically defined by their faith in Christ Jesus.

Social Standing

The second implication of being members of God's people is found in Galatians 3:28: "There is neither Jew nor Greek, there is neither slave nor free, there is no male and female, for you are all one in Christ Jesus." This is a most interesting verse, and it has rightly been celebrated in scholarship and in the church as a radical statement. Once again, we need to attend to the context of what is said. In Galatians 3 Paul discusses membership in the people of God, showing us what it means and what is required to be a member of the family of Abraham. The declaration in 3:28 is quite astonishing, overturning the conceptions of many in the ancient world. We have already seen in our discussion of circumcision and the law that whether one was a Jew or a Gentile, a Jew or a Greek, was not the fundamental issue. What matters is whether one belongs to Christ. Paul does not limit himself here to the Jew-Gentile issue but goes on to speak of both slaves and free. One's social standing, whether one is of the social elite, is irrelevant with respect to membership in the people of God. In other words, and as we shall see shortly, all members of the community are brothers and sisters. One doesn't relate to others based on social status or one's position in society but based on one's faith in Jesus Christ. As has often been pointed out, Paul develops new kinship categories, a new idea of what it means to be family. We can see from this how later in history, even by the second century, Christians identified believers as a third race.[2]

Paul doesn't only speak of there being no more Jew or Greek or slave or free but also that there is no more male or female. Of course, we have to keep in mind once again that he is speaking of access to salvation, of whether salvation is limited to males or includes females. It is quite interesting that circumcision is no longer the entrance point into the people of God since circumcision as an initiation rite is limited to males. It is fascinating to observe that baptism is mentioned in the verse just prior to Galatians 3:27, and baptism, which is the initiation right into the church of Christ, applies equally to males and females. The significance of this, even if Paul doesn't comment on it explicitly, seems evident. The people of God are no longer marked by the male head of the family, and the patriarchal nature of the people of God shifts to a new kind of equality. We can put it this way: now each person makes an individual decision whether to receive the initiation right into the people of God. Of course, this applies as well to slaves and free. Slaves were counted as members of the Christian church, members of Abraham's family, because of their faith—not simply because their masters were believers. The same now applies to females. Conversely, slaves or females may be believers while masters or husbands are outside of the family of Abraham. Each person now stands before God on his or her own, though we should not draw from this that the corporate life of the church isn't necessary. Paul's understanding of salvation has social consequences that were quite explosive. Jews and Gentiles, males and females, and slaves and free related to one another in dramatically new ways in the church of Jesus Christ.

The social implications of Paul's teaching, then, should not be neglected, and that is a larger topic that can't be explored fully here. At the same time, we must be careful so that we understand Paul on his own terms and in his own context. A superficial reading might lead us to conclude that maleness and femaleness don't exist at all, as if Paul abolishes such distinctions altogether. The same mistake could be said

[2] See Aristides, *Apology* 2.

about being a Jew or Gentile, or a slave or free. It is clear when we read all of Paul's letters that he doesn't teach that one's ethnic background is cancelled as if it no longer exists. Paul prays specifically in Romans 9 for the Jews to be saved and often distinguishes between Jews and Gentiles in his letters. Along the same lines, Paul gives particular instructions for masters and slaves and their responsibilities differ (Eph. 6:5–9; Col. 3:22–4:1). Paul recognized and affirmed that social relations continued to exist in society. We should not conclude from this that Paul endorsed or commended slavery. Slavery is an evil human institution that was regulated in the New Testament without ever being applauded.[3] When the church of Jesus Christ has social influence, it should move to abolish the institution. We have some indications of this impulse in the New Testament since Paul encourages those who can obtain freedom from slavery to do so (1 Cor. 7:21).

Nor does Paul conclude that there are no differences between men and women. If there was no such thing as male or female whatsoever, then Paul would have no objection to same-sex relationships, but it is clear that Paul believed that homosexual relationships were sinful (Rom. 1:26–27; 1 Cor. 6:9; 1 Tim. 1:9).[4] Similarly, he believed that there were different roles for husbands and wives, and Paul put limitations on what women could do in the assembly (Eph. 5:22–33; Col. 3:18–19; Titus 2:5). For instance, he believed that teaching and leadership roles in the churches should be restricted to men (1 Tim. 2:11–14; cf. 1 Cor. 14:33–36). All of this is very controversial in our present day, and it isn't my purpose or the aim of this book to delve into these matters in detail.[5] I would simply say that the most natural way of interpreting Paul

---

[3] Readers should consult the excellent book by Murray J. Harris, *Slave of Christ: A New Testament Metaphor for Total Devotion to Christ*, NSBT 9 (Downers Grove, IL: InterVarsity Press, 1999).

[4] For further support, see Thomas R. Schreiner, "A New Perspective on Homosexuality," *Them* 31 (2006) 62–75; Thomas R. Schreiner, "New Trajectories and Old Patterns: Hermeneutics and Same Sex Advocacy," *Journal for Global Christianity* 2 (2016): 48–63, http://trainingleadersinternational.org/jgc/61/new-trajectories-and-old-patterns-hermeneutics-and-same-sex-advocacy.

[5] For a defense of what is said here, see Thomas R. Schreiner, "Women in Ministry: Another Complementarian Perspective," in *Two Views on Women in Ministry*, rev. ed., ed. James R.

is to read him to say that such differences between males and females continue in the church of Jesus Christ.

We face two dangers here. We can underestimate or overestimate the radical nature of Paul's teaching. There are certainly social implications that can be drawn from Paul's teaching since soteriology and life in community must not be segregated from each other. Paul's soteriological understanding indeed affected life in the community of the redeemed. There is no place for devaluing or discriminating against others. Historical social barriers have been erased with the salvation that has arrived in Christ Jesus. A new community has been realized where all are brothers and sisters, where everyone plays a part, where everyone is equally significant and valuable, where no one is scorned or slighted because of gender, ethnic background, or social status. At the same time, there is the danger of reading Paul in light of the culture of our day, imposing on him a perspective that is quite alien to his own vision of the people of God. All of Paul's teaching must be consulted to obtain a wholistic conception of the new family of Abraham. Of course, the task isn't easy, and careful exegesis and perceptive theological insight are needed to do justice to all that Paul says.

Social Implications of the Gospel

The Incident at Antioch

We see the social ramifications of Paul's soteriology in the incident at Antioch (Gal. 2:11–14). Peter and the other Jewish Christians, including Barnabas, were enjoying table fellowship with Gentile believers. Scholars debate what this fellowship looked like. Some think Peter and the others observed some minimal Jewish dietary requirements that were also acceptable to the Gentile believers.[6] This is an intriguing suggestion, and

---

Beck, Counterpoints (Grand Rapids, MI: Zondervan, 2005), 263–322; Thomas Schreiner, "1 Timothy 2:9–15: A Dialogue with Scholarship," in *Women in the Church: An Analysis and Application of 1 Timothy 2:9–15*, 3rd ed., ed. Andreas Köstenberger and Thomas R. Schreiner (Wheaton, IL: Crossway, 2016), 163–225. See also Kevin DeYoung, *Women in the Church: A Short, Biblical, Practical Introduction* (Wheaton, IL: Crossway, 2021).

6 J. D. G. Dunn, "The Incident at Antioch (Gal 2:11–18)," *JSNT* 18 (1983): 3–57.

it can't be ruled out as impossible, but there is no evidence for such a scenario.[7] Others suggest that Jews and Gentiles were eating together, but they weren't necessarily eating the same food.[8] On this reading, the Jews may have continued to observe the purity rules found in the torah (Lev. 11 and Deut. 14). Once again, this is possible, but we have no textual indication that this was the state of affairs.

It is more likely that the Jews were eating with the Gentiles and were not observing the dietary prescriptions found in the torah. This understanding of the situation fits with Mark 7:19 where Jesus declared all foods clean.[9] The connection between Mark and Galatians is strengthened if Mark wrote his Gospel at Peter's impetus. The early tradition traces Mark's composition of his Gospel to Petrine influence, and I believe this tradition is historically reliable. Even if Mark didn't write under Peter's influence, Peter was present when Jesus uttered these words and thus knew firsthand what Jesus taught. Peter probably had drawn the conclusion (in part from Jesus's teaching) that all foods were clean, and thus he would feel free to have table fellowship with Gentiles, even eating food with them that was formerly deemed to be unclean.

Such a reading harmonizes as well with Acts 10:1–11:18. Luke recounts the story of Peter's encounter with Cornelius. What is germane for our purposes is the vision Peter received where a great sheet was lowered from heaven and Peter was instructed to kill and eat the creatures in the sheet. Peter objected since the animals in the sheet included creatures that were unclean and forbidden by the torah. God, however, assured him that such foods were now clean and permitted. The vision was shown to Peter three times, certifying that it was clearly the will of God. Once again, the relation to the text in Galatians is clear. Peter is told in Acts that all foods are clean and permissible, and presumably it

---

7   Dan Cohn-Sherbok, "Some Reflections on James Dunn's 'The Incident at Antioch (Gal 2:11–18),'" *JSNT* 18 (1983): 68–74; J. L. Houlden, "A Response to J. D. G. Dunn," *JSNT* 18 (1983): 58–67.
8   Peter J. Tomson, *Paul and the Jewish Law: Halakah in the Letters of the Apostle to the Gentiles*, Compendia Rerum Iudaicarum ad Novum Testamentum 3/1 (Minneapolis: Fortress, 1990), 227–36.
9   This is a Markan comment on the import of Jesus's teaching.

was such an experience that shaped his actions at Antioch where he ate at table with Gentiles. All this leads me to think that Peter actually ate food that was according to Old Testament law unclean because Peter had been convinced that such food was now acceptable.

As we know, however, this was not the end of the story. We read in Galatians 2:11–14 that some men from James came to Peter with particular instructions. Unfortunately, we aren't told precisely what they said. Paul breezes over the details in an extreme hurry so that the story lacks the color and fullness we would love to have. It seems quite likely, however, that the men from James told Peter that he was putting Jewish Christians (perhaps in Jerusalem and Judea) at a great risk in eating unclean food with Gentiles. The report of such activity by Christians would reach unbelieving Jews in these regions quickly and would provoke outrage and perhaps even persecution. We can only speculate, but perhaps James said that the actions of Peter and other Jewish Christians was not advisable given the explosive political situation in Judea.[10]

Whatever was said, we know that Peter ceased eating with the Gentiles, and the rest of the Jews followed his example. What must have particularly grieved and galled Paul were the actions of Barnabas, his partner on the first missionary journey (Acts 13–14). Barnabas didn't follow Paul's example but Peter's. Peter's influence brought to an abrupt end the table fellowship between Jews and Gentiles. Paul responded by reproving Peter publicly, which was justified since the sin was a public matter and had public consequences. Everyone present knew what Peter had done, and his actions had a tidal-wave effect, sweeping everyone with him. Thus, Paul had to act quickly and publicly before the unity of the church and the gospel proclaimed by him were destroyed. Paul instantly saw that "the truth of the gospel" was at stake (Gal. 2:14). Even if Peter did not intend it, he was in effect communicating that one had to observe the purity rules of table fellowship for salvation. Paul uses the

---

10 Robert Jewett, "The Agitators and the Galatian Congregation," in *The Galatians Debate: Contemporary Issues in Rhetorical and Historical Interpretation*, ed. Mark D. Nanos (Peabody, MA: Hendrickson, 2002), 334–47.

verb "force" (*anankazō*) in 2:14. This is the same verb used in 2:3 of the false brothers who tried to "force" Titus as a Gentile to be circumcised, and it is the same verb used of the Jewish teachers who were trying to "force" the Galatians to be circumcised (6:12). Peter's defection, then, was not a minor matter since he was advocating, even if inadvertently, the same course of action promoted by those proclaiming a false gospel. The difference, of course, was that Peter acted hypocritically (2:14) and not according to his true convictions.

The point I am making, however, is that the gospel has social implications. By refusing to eat with the Gentiles, Peter was in effect denying the gospel! If someone were to say that eating with someone is a minor matter, Paul disagrees! By refusing table fellowship, Peter was suggesting, whether he intended to or not, that the Gentiles weren't truly Christians. He was erecting afresh the barrier between Jews and Greeks that had been torn down through the death of Christ. We cannot say, then, that the gospel should be restricted to theology since for Paul theology affects everyday life, including whom you are willing to eat with at breakfast, lunch, and dinner. We have to think carefully, of course, about social implications for our own world, and we must be constrained and directed by the biblical witness and careful theological reflection instead of constructing a social agenda that conforms to current societal mores.

Controversy over Titus

The social implications of the gospel are also reflected in the account in Galatians 2:1–10. We read about Paul's visit to Jerusalem where he met with the pillar apostles—Peter, James, and John. Much ink has been spilled about when this meeting occurred and whether it represents the same meeting recorded in Acts 15. I incline to the south Galatian hypothesis, seeing the meeting as taking place earlier than the one in Acts 15 so that Galatians 2:1–10 matches Acts 11:27–30. Still, the timing of the meeting isn't the main concern. Paul tells us that he brought Titus along on the trip and (as we have noticed before) that false brothers sparked a controversy by insisting that Titus be circumcised (Gal.

2:3–5). Paul celebrates the fact that the pillar apostles took his side in the whole debate so that Titus was not compelled to be circumcised. We saw earlier that the independence and truth of Paul's gospel were ratified in this account. But there is another facet of the story that should be noticed. The agreement of the pillar apostles with Paul testifies to the unity of the early church.

Peter and Paul, of course, differed over whether one should eat unclean food with the Gentiles (Gal. 2:11–14), but, as I argued earlier, there are good reasons for thinking that Peter repented and agreed with Paul. Thus, the unity between Paul and the pillar apostles in 2:1–10 wasn't a sham. They truly agreed on the content of the gospel, and such agreement is most significant. The unity of the church is grounded in truth, in the truth of the gospel. The church is a new family, and believers are brothers and sisters in the gospel (1:2; 6:18). But even in 1:2, where Paul refers to the brothers who were with him, he subtly intimates that their family relationship is rooted in the truth of the gospel. Paul likely mentions the brothers with him to suggest that they, in contrast to the Galatians, were holding firm to the gospel Paul proclaimed. The brothers with him were brothers in the truth, and the Galatians needed a course correction so that they were aligned once again with the gospel proclaimed by the church worldwide.

We see, then, that the unity of the church is a central Pauline theme, but it isn't a unity that compromises the truth of the gospel. What Paul teaches reminds us of John 17 where Jesus prays for the unity of the church, but the unity is rooted in truth. Some desire unity today but are willing to compromise on the truth of the gospel to achieve such unity, and Paul would never make such a move. At the same time, there is a danger of being overly rigorous where we demand detailed agreement with every doctrinal opinion we hold. Working this out in today's world, of course, is incredibly complex. But we can at least agree that we should strive for unity and that, if there are divisions, they should be rooted in commitment to the truth of the gospel.

Friendship

We see another instance of the social implications of the gospel in Galatians 4:12–20. The text is fascinating because it is deeply personal and relational. Paul hasn't forgotten about the truth of the gospel, and he exhorts the Galatians to remain faithful by reminding them of his friendship with them. He recalls "the good old days" when he first proclaimed the gospel to them and they received Paul "as an angel of God, as Christ Jesus" (4:14). Indeed, their love for Paul was so intense that they were even willing, so to speak, to gouge out their eyes for his sake. Their warm reception of Paul was even more remarkable because he was afflicted with some kind of sickness, and Paul's illness could have been so repulsive that they would refuse to accept him.

The warm memories of the past, however, were in danger of being erased with the arrival of the agitators. Apparently, Paul's insistence on "telling you the truth" (4:16), the truth of the gospel, imperiled their friendship. Paul can't imagine, however, any friendship that isn't built on the truth. The Jewish teachers were waving an olive branch before the Galatians, but the motive of these teachers was suspect. They weren't passionate for the truth of the gospel. Instead, they were narcissistic and self-obsessed. They wanted the friendship of the Galatians for their own sake, for their own reputation, for their own egos. Paul longed to be friends with the Galatians for their benefit and for the sake of the gospel. The Jewish teachers pretended to be friends, but they were actually only concerned about themselves. Paul's desire, on the other hand, was not that he would be exalted but that Christ would be formed in them (4:19).

Conclusion

We see in this chapter that the church is united because we are all sons and daughters of Abraham through faith in Jesus Christ. Believers in Jesus are the Israel of God, part of the family of Abraham, whether they are Jews or Gentiles. Remarkably, the social divisions that marked the ancient world have come tumbling down. In the church of Jesus Christ whether one is a Jew or a Gentile, slave or free, male or female is no longer decisive. All people everywhere have equal access to salvation. The social implications of what Paul teaches are indeed revolutionary, but at the same time we must beware of letting current social agendas color how we understand Paul. We must read all of Paul and everything he says on these matters to construct an authentic portrait of his own view. The incident at Antioch (Gal. 2:11–14) also teaches us that the unity of the church can't be segregated from everyday life. The refusal to have table fellowship with the Gentiles was actually a denial of the gospel. The unity and friendship that characterized the early Christians was a unity rooted in the truth, in the gospel itself.

8

Life in the Spirit

Introduction

Paul in Galatians emphasizes that justification doesn't come through the works of the law but through faith in Jesus Christ. The focus on grace could lead us to think that the transformation and new life of believers wasn't a major concern. But we see from Galatians 5:13–6:10 that the new life of believers was also important. Some have maintained that Paul didn't prepare the Galatians adequately for their new life as Christians,[1] but this is quite unlikely. We read in 5:21 that Paul had told them in advance that those who practice the works of the flesh will not inherit the kingdom. If Paul had warned them about this danger previously, it is clear that he was concerned from the beginning about the moral life of the Galatians.

We have to seek, then, a better explanation for the admonitions we find in this section. It is more likely that Paul anticipates a possible overreaction to his teaching on grace. He realizes that the Galatians might respond to the freedom from the law in a way that subverts the gospel. They might receive Paul's message as an invitation to live licentiously. Such a response would constitute a misunderstanding of the gospel of grace, as if it promoted a life bereft of righteousness. Thus,

---

1 Han Dieter Betz, *Galatians: A Commentary on Paul's Letter to the Churches in Galatia*, Hermeneia (Philadelphia: Fortress, 1979), 8–9, 273.

Paul explicates for them what the new life looks like for those who have embraced the good news of the gospel.

Life in the Spirit

The life of freedom is a life lived by the power of the Holy Spirit, and the Spirit plays a major role in the letter.[2] We read in Galatians 5:16 that believers who are justified by grace are to walk by the Spirit and to resist fleshly desires. The metaphor of walking signifies that Christians depend every step of the way on the Holy Spirit for help in living in a way that pleases God. The Spirit empowers believers so that they do not yield to fleshly desires. We see from 5:17 that the call to live by the Spirit isn't easy. A battle rages between the Spirit and the flesh, and the fundamental opposition between the Spirit and the flesh is highlighted. The flesh here represents what believers are in Adam, the unregenerate nature of human beings. The flesh cannot be restricted to the body but represents human beings in all their fallenness. How to interpret what Paul is saying in 5:17 is quite difficult. It can be read as if there were a stalemate between the Spirit and the flesh so that Christians live in a kind of no-man's-land. Such a solution isn't convincing. Intense conflict characterizes Christian existence, but Paul's optimistic view of the Christian life in the rest of Galatians 5–6 rules out the notion that we have a mere stalemate. In some ways, this verse reminds us of Romans 7:14–25 where the struggle with sin is described so poignantly. The text can be compared to Romans 7 in that the conflict that characterizes Christian experience is featured. I suggest that we should read Galatians 5:17 to say that the Spirit curbs the passions and lusts that flow from human beings. Paul isn't talking, of course, about perfection, as if human beings were entirely free from sin. Still, what predominates is the newness that characterizes our lives as believers.

This fits with Galatians 5:18 where those who are led by the Spirit are not under the law. We have already seen in our study that those who are under the law are under the power of sin. The optimistic character

---

2 See particularly here Jarvis W. Williams, *The Spirit, Ethics, and Eternal Life: Paul's Vision for the Christian Life* (Downers Grove, IL: IVP Academic, 2023).

of Paul's view of the Christian life shines through here. Those who are governed and directed by the Holy Spirit live in a dramatically new way. The opponents claimed that the moral life would only be enabled by the law, but Paul contends that those who rely on the law for righteousness actually are giving sin a platform. The fundamental need of human beings isn't for moral instruction but power, and that power comes from the Holy Spirit. Thus believers must not put themselves under the law; they are called upon to give themselves to the Holy Spirit and to allow the Spirit to govern and direct their lives. When that happens, believers will live in a way that pleases God.

Fruit of the Spirit and Works of the Flesh

Paul contrasts the fruit of the Spirit with the works of the flesh (Gal. 5:19–23). We should note first of all that the fruit comes from the Spirit. This means that the new life of believers is supernatural, that it has a divine origin, that it can't be produced by the moral effort of human beings in their own strength. At the same time, the listing of the works of the flesh clarifies what it means and what it looks like to give oneself over to evil (5:19–21). Paul remarks that the works of the flesh are evident. They are not mysterious and difficult to identify, as if one needed some kind of special insight to discern what is from the flesh and what is from the Spirit. Identifying the works of the flesh isn't limited to the spiritual elite but is obvious to all who have moral sense.

The works of the flesh can be divided into four categories. First, three different terms are used for sexual sin (Gal. 5:19). Those who engage in sexual sin are energized by their selfish will, by which they use others for their own pleasure instead of living to help others flourish. Sexual sin, according to Paul, defiles, defaces, and deforms human beings. Their lack of restraint, their lack of control over their bodies, shows that they are living only for themselves. Second, two terms are used for idolatry (Gal. 5:20). Idolatry and sorcery represent an attempt to manipulate life without submission to the rule and sovereignty of God. Human beings turn to false gods because they are worshiping the creature rather than the Creator (Rom. 1:25).

Third, and most remarkably, eight sins are listed from the social realm (Gal. 5:20–21). Sins like jealousy, hatred, fighting, fits of anger, dissension, and bitterness are named. The remarkable emphasis on social sins suggests that this was Paul's major concern in the Galatian congregation. We also learn from the concentration on social sins that the flesh can't be restricted to sins of the body. In fact, the focus is on sins that alienate human beings from one another. The selfishness of human beings manifests itself in quarreling and in mutual suspicion and dislike. Churches may be doctrinally faithful and yet be torn to pieces by gossip, slander, and hatred. Fourth, the last two sins have to do with drunkenness and wild parties (5:21). In such situations human beings often lose control of their faculties, opening the door for behavior that inflicts damage on others. Furthermore, those who give themselves to such a way of life reveal that their lives are governed by their own pleasures and desires. Instead of depending on God for joy, they give themselves to stimulants.

If the works of the flesh are obvious, so is the fruit of the Spirit. It is difficult to know if the singular "fruit" is important exegetically in contrast to the plural "fruits." If the former is intentional, Paul emphasizes the unity of the fruit of the Spirit, indicating that they can't be parceled out into nine different fruits as if we work on just one fruit at a time. Even if the singular "fruit" should not be pressed for meaning, the fruit of the Spirit can't be isolated in such a way. When one is walking in and led by the Spirit, all these qualities exist in the lives of believers.

We are not surprised that the first fruit listed is love since love is the most important evidence of life in the Spirit. If we take a bit of a side road, we recall that those who love fulfill God's law (Gal. 5:13–14; cf. Rom. 13:8–10). Plus, love in Paul's thought binds together all the virtues (Col. 3:14). What the Corinthians really needed in their arguments over food offered to idols (1 Cor. 8:1–3) and the contention over spiritual gifts (1 Cor. 13:1–13) was love. The first quality named in Paul's virtue list in Romans 12:9–21 is love. Paul also emphasizes in Galatians that faith expresses itself in love (Gal. 5:6). The fundamental command for husbands is to love and cherish their wives (Eph. 5:25–29; Col. 3:19), and the entire Christian life can be described as a call to walk in love (Eph. 5:2). When Paul prays for the Philippians, he asks that their love would increase along with discernment and knowledge (Phil. 1:9; cf. 2 Thess. 3:5). The goal of Paul's ministry is that the lives of believers would be characterized by love (1 Tim. 1:5).

Some of the fruit mentioned in Galatians 5:22 is another way of describing love. For instance, in 1 Corinthians 13:4 love is called patient and kind, and patience and kindness are listed as fruit of the Spirit as well. Faithfulness and self-control (Gal. 5:23) can be distinguished from love; but there is certainly a close connection since those who love are loyal and those who lack self-control tend to be reckless and undisciplined, spreading misery wherever they go. Not all of the fruit of the Spirit can be equated with love. For instance, joy and peace aren't the same thing as love, but they stand in contrast to the crabbiness and anxiety that weigh down our lives. Those who are walking and being governed by the Spirit are joyful and contented.

Interestingly, Paul says that there is no law against the fruit of the Spirit (Gal. 5:23). His point is probably that the law can't produce a life that is beautiful and pleasing to God. Only the Holy Spirit can transform, shape, and empower human beings so that they live in a way that God intended human beings to live from the beginning.

March in Step with the Spirit

We have seen that believers are urged to walk in the Spirit, are directed by the Spirit, and will produce the fruit of the Spirit. In Galatians 5:25–26 life in the Spirit continues to be rehearsed. Believers are exhorted to "keep in step with the Spirit" (5:25), and the verb here (*stoicheō*) has the sense of marching in accord with the Spirit, taking the orders of the Spirit. The call to keep in step with God's Spirit is rooted in the indicative work of God through Jesus Christ. Those exhorted to march in step with the Spirit are those who have new life by the Spirit. Paul is not appealing to human autonomy or human strength, as if we had the potential and capacity to keep in step with the Spirit. Only those who already live in the Spirit have the ability to keep in step with the Spirit.

We have a clear example here of the indicative and the imperative where the indicative is the foundation and basis for the imperative. In other words, the imperative can only be carried out because of the indicative, but it must be carried out because of the indicative. The instructions to follow the Spirit's lead are never for Paul ethereal or abstract. He immediately communicates what life in the Spirit looks like in everyday life. Those who follow the Spirit will not permit a spirit of conceit and pride to rule in their lives. Nor will they engage in behavior that challenges and provokes other people, which means that they will not be argumentative and contentious. At the same time, they will not fall prey to envy so that they bear grudges against those who are flourishing in their lives. What Paul says here reminds us of a verse that we skipped in our study of the Spirit. In Galatians 5:15 the readers are warned not to bite and devour one another. These are the activities of animals who consume their prey. The word "bite" (*daknō*) is particularly interesting because it is used regularly of snakes that bite human beings (Gen. 49:17; Num. 21:6, 8, 9; Deut. 8:15; Eccl. 10:8, 11; Amos 5:19; 9:3; Jer. 8:17; Sir. 21:2). Biting and critical words that tear down others are satanic. Believers are not walking in the Spirit when they use their tongues to attack, tear down, and demonize others. The social dimension of walking in the Spirit comes to the forefront again.

Corporate and Individual Responsibility in the Spirit

Paul continues to reflect on life in the Spirit in Galatians 6:1–10. He refers to those "who are spiritual" and have responsibility "to restore" those who have fallen into sin (6:1). We might think that the spiritual ones refer to elite Christians, to believers who live particularly godly lives. But the emphasis on the Spirit in 5:16–6:10 leads us to another conclusion. All believers without exception are spiritual, which means that all believers are indwelt by and empowered by the Holy Spirit. Thus, the admonition isn't restricted to part of the congregation. On the other hand, the admonition to restore those who have fallen into a trespass reveals that life in the Spirit is complicated, that those who have the Spirit may wander into sin. Similarly, those who are spiritual must also be on guard against temptation since sin is deceptive and attacks in ways that we don't anticipate. Restoring others who have fallen may become a platform for pride or for being tempted by other sins that crop up unawares. Thus, believers are admonished to restore with gentleness those who have transgressed, linking back to 5:23 where gentleness is a fruit of the Spirit. Harshness, arrogance, and disdain are to be avoided at all costs.

John Barclay in his important book on obedience in Galatians remarks on the interplay between the individual and the community that characterizes Paul's exhortations in the last part of the letter.[3] This dynamic shows up in Galatians 6:1–5. Concern for others is reflected in the call to bear one another's burdens, showing that life in the Spirit is communitarian and social. Such a reminder is needed since evangelical Christians, especially in the West, tend to privatize what it means to live faithfully as believers so that individual piety can be sundered from life in the church. At the same time, we must beware of thinking only in communitarian terms and neglecting individual responsibility. Paul warns believers once again of pride (6:3), which manifests itself when we think that we are something, although in reality we are nothing before God. Perhaps Paul gives this admonition right after telling us to carry one another's burdens because we are tempted to think when we help others that we are quite gifted. It is striking that Paul returns again (see 5:26) to the danger of pride. I am reminded of C. S. Lewis and the explosive chapter on pride in his book *Mere Christianity*. Lewis remarks that "if you think you are not conceited, it means you are very conceited indeed."[4] Perhaps we could rephrase this: if you think you are not tempted by conceit, you are very likely to be a victim of it.

Paul has been emphasizing our corporate responsibility to one another, but then in Galatians 6:4 he shifts the focus to the individual. As believers we are summoned to test and examine our own lives. We are to carry the burdens of others, and that is part of our task and calling

---

3   John M. G. Barclay, *Obeying the Truth: Paul's Ethics in Galatians* (Minneapolis: Fortress, 1988), 149–50.
4   C. S. Lewis, *Mere Christianity* (New York: HarperOne, 1952), 128.

as believers. Paul may anticipate a false conclusion from community life. We need each other, and we rely in so many ways on the help of others. Still, at the end of the day each one of us is responsible for his or her own life. We can't excuse the weaknesses and sins we have committed by claiming that others didn't help us as they should have. We must examine our own lives objectively to discern whether we are really following the Lord.

Paul then turns to the final day, to the day of reward. Speaking of believers boasting sounds strange, especially since Paul claims in Galatians 6:14 that he only boasts in the cross of Christ, and yet here he speaks of boasting in oneself. It is hard to imagine a conception more alien to the message of Galatians. In fact, the false teachers are indicted for boasting (6:13). What we need to remember is that Paul is a coherent writer, and he doesn't contradict what he writes a few verses later. Nor does he contradict the message of the entire letter, which is that human beings can't boast of their works before God, as if their works could accomplish salvation. The boasting Paul has in mind is eschatological, a boasting that will take place on the day of judgment—the day of final reward. Elsewhere Paul uses the word "boasting" to refer to final reward (1 Cor. 9:15–16; 2 Cor. 1:14; Phil. 2:16; 1 Thess. 2:19). So too here the final reward believers will receive is in view. We notice that he emphasizes that each of us will be rewarded individually and personally. The reward will not be based on what others do but what we ourselves have done. We would misinterpret the word "boasting" if we understood it as a reception of a reward based on our autonomous work. Our boasting is a result of God's gracious and transforming work in us, and yet at the same time we are rewarded for how we have lived. We see the delicate tension between divine sovereignty and human responsibility. We find a similar tension in Philippians 2:12–13 where Paul teaches that we work out our own salvation, but in the final analysis our work is the result of God's work in us. God gives us the desire to do his will and the energy to carry it out.

The emphasis on the individual continues in Galatians 6:5 where we find a proverbial-like statement that each person will carry his own load. This could be understood as referring to what should happen in everyday life in the sense that each of us should take responsibility for our own actions. This proverbial-like saying would stand in contrast, or perhaps better in tandem, with 6:2 where we are to carry one another's burdens. More likely, however, the future tense verb "will carry" (*bastasei*) doesn't refer to this life but to the final judgment. We find the same verb in 5:10: "The one who is troubling you will bear [*bastasei*] the penalty, whoever he is." There is no doubt in the latter verse that the reference is to the final judgment, and the same verb in the same tense in 6:5 probably points forward to the future day. I suggested above that 6:4 refers to the last day as well. If this is the case, Paul calls on believers to assist and help one another in this life, while recognizing that at the final judgment each one of us will stand individually before God, and we will be evaluated and rewarded for what we have done.

Generosity by the Spirit

The interplay between corporate and individual responsibility continues in Galatians 6:6–10. Those who are taught the word—that is, those who are being instructed—are to support financially those who are teaching them. The individual who benefits from the teaching of God's word should see to it that those teaching have sufficient resources to live their lives. The notion that teachers should be supported is a common theme in Paul's letters (1 Cor. 9:1–14; 1 Tim. 5:17–18). It is evident that there are teachers or leaders in the community who had a special responsibility to instruct the saints, and this fits with other references in the Pauline corpus (Rom. 12:7–8; 1 Cor. 12:28; 16:15–16; Eph. 4:11; Phil. 1:1; 1 Thess. 5:12–13; 1 Tim. 3:7; 5:17; Titus 1:5–9).

Paul zeros in on the responsibility of individual believers, using the singular in Galatians 6:7–8. The image of sowing and reaping describes the activity demanded of believers. Elsewhere in Paul sowing and reaping are used in financial contexts (1 Cor. 9:11; 2 Cor. 9:6, 10). Given Galatians 6:6, it seems that such a notion continues here, and the necessity of generosity continues through 6:10. Still, we should probably not limit sowing and reaping to generosity, and thus it probably captures the whole of our lives as well. In 6:7 the seriousness of the exhortation is underscored as Paul warns the readers about self-deceit and the danger of mocking God in the way they live. Once again, the final judgment seems to be in mind. Everyone will reap what they sow. In a letter that emphasizes God's grace and engages in a polemic against the works of the law, it is really quite remarkable how Paul emphasizes so ardently the necessity of a moral life. Galatians 6:8 adds a very important explanation. Those who will be corrupted will be judged because they have sown to the flesh. They have lived for their own selfish advantage instead of doing the will of God. We are also reminded that those who will receive an eschatological reward, which is described as eternal life, do so by the Spirit. Human beings do not have the capacity for righteous living apart from God's dynamic Spirit who strengthens us in every good work. Furthermore, there is no doubt that one's eschatological destiny is at stake since Paul contrasts "corruption" with "eternal life" (6:8). Those who give in to the flesh will face end-time corruption—final judgment—while those who sow to the Spirit will enjoy life in the age to come. God's judgment is fitting since those who sow to the flesh reap what the flesh gives—namely, judgment—whereas those who sow to the Spirit reap what the Spirit gives—namely, eternal life.

The difficulty of life in this world is acknowledged as Paul recognizes in Galatians 6:9 that believers may be tempted to grow weary and cease doing what is good. Doing good probably continues the theme of helping others financially, though once again it probably has a broader meaning as well, referring to doing good in general. The motivation for continuing to do good is the final judgment, which is again described as a future reaping. Sowing continues as long as life lasts, but a day of reaping is coming when believers will be rewarded for the good they have done while those who have given themselves to evil will face judgment. Paul rounds off this whole discussion in Galatians 6:10: life on earth is a time of "opportunity" (*kairos*), a time to make our lives count forever. He actually plays on the same word that is used in Galatians 6:9 ("season" in ESV); but in the latter verse it refers to the judgment day, to the final time. We also find in Ephesians

5:16 and Colossians 4:5 that the term can mean an opportunity, as Paul encourages believers to make use of every opportunity to do what is good. In Galatians 6:10 believers are exhorted to do good to "everyone," which includes unbelievers. Once again, financial assistance is particularly in view, showing that concern for poverty and the needs of people animated the early Christians. Still, assistance is to be parceled out especially to the saints, to fellow believers, to what Paul calls "the household of faith" (6:10).

The focus on fellow believers fits with 1 Timothy 5:3–16 where Paul gives exhortations about widows who need financial help. He emphasizes that families, if they have the resources, should help widows before the latter ask the church for assistance. The church should only help if the family doesn't have the resources or the widow doesn't have any family left. We see, then, a structure or pattern for financial assistance. Circles of responsibility are established. First, families should provide, if possible, for their own needs. Second, the church should provide for the needs of fellow members. Third, if there are sufficient resources, then churches should help others outside of the community of faith.

Conclusion

The new life of believers is life in the Spirit, a life where we walk in the Spirit, are directed by the Spirit, produce the fruit of the Spirit, march in step with the Spirit, and sow to the Spirit. The Spirit is a transforming presence in believers, radically reshaping and reformatting their lives. Instead of the law being the impetus for change, reformation occurs supernaturally through the power of the Holy Spirit. Life in the Spirit isn't an abstraction, for we see the difference in everyday life, particularly in how we treat other people. This is simply another way of saying that life in the Spirit is marked by love, by concern for the well-being of others. The new life of believers has both an individual and corporate character. It is corporate in that we share life with others and help and assist them on their journey, and Paul particularly emphasizes that we care for others financially. At the same time, the new life is individual in that we stand before God ultimately accountable for the decisions we make. No one else can be blamed if our lives do not match what God requires. But such a calling brings us back to where we started in this chapter: we cannot live in a way that pleases God on our own, which is why we need the Holy Spirit.

Epilogue

We have been on a journey in this book, a journey in which we dropped down into the lives of the Galatians in the first century AD. We heard about their lives through the lens of the apostle Paul, discovering that they embraced his gospel initially. When some Jewish teachers arrived, however, teaching that they must observe the law and be circumcised for salvation, their faith tottered. Indeed, they began to wonder whether Paul's gospel was faithful to Old Testament revelation. Paul strikes back by emphasizing the truth and independence of his gospel, informing the readers that the apostles in Jerusalem also ratified and validated his gospel.

The Pauline gospel is radically eschatological and apocalyptic. Circumcision is no longer required because the new age has come with apocalyptic power in the crucifixion and resurrection of Jesus Christ. The problem with the Galatians is that they didn't know what time it was; the new age had dawned and they were still living in the old age. It was as if they had slumbered and didn't know that a new era had arrived. Because of this the Galatians were tempted to live under the law—the covenant given to Israel at Mount Sinai. But the age of the law, the time in which the Mosaic covenant was in force, had passed away since the new covenant had arrived.

As Paul remarks, the Galatians were bewitched, dazzled, and under a spell so that they didn't understand the cross. By insisting on circumcision they were in effect saying that Christ died for nothing. One can't have it both ways: either the cross of Christ or circumcision brings one into the people of God. Embracing circumcision meant one rejected Christ and all his benefits. In promoting the law, the agitators were promoting a different way of justification before God, claiming that one's works, one's performance, one's achievements, could lead to eschatological vindication. By way of contrast, Paul insisted on the truth of the gospel, which is that righteousness before God only comes through faith in Jesus Christ as the crucified and risen one. We are not right before God by working for God but by receiving free forgiveness. The family of Abraham, then, doesn't consist of those who are Jewish, of those who are circumcised and keep the law. The family of Abraham is radically redrawn around the person of Jesus Christ. He is the true offspring of Abraham so that all of those who are members of Abraham's family, all those who are the true Israel, belong to Jesus Christ.

The arrival of the new age in Jesus means that previous social distinctions are no longer relevant for salvation. New life in Jesus doesn't only change our relationship to God but also our relationship to one another. One's ethnic background, social class, or gender is not primary. What matters is whether one belongs to Jesus and whether we treat one another as family, as equal members of the people of God.

We might think that the moral life, the ethical life, doesn't matter for Paul since salvation comes by faith instead of through the works of the law. But those who put their faith in Jesus Christ have received the Holy Spirit, and the Holy Spirit transforms God's people so that they live in a way that pleases him, not in their own strength but through the transforming power of the Holy Spirit. Paul doesn't teach a gospel of free grace that leads to antinomianism or licentiousness. He teaches a gospel of free grace that unleashes God's power and his Spirit so that we follow the pattern of life modeled by Jesus Christ, a life where we love others in thought, word, and deed. By the power of the Spirit, believers keep the law of Christ (not perfectly, of course), which is nothing other than the law of love, and in this way they fulfill the true purpose of the law that God gave to Moses.

Appendix

A Review of *Paul and the Gift* by John M. G. Barclay

John Barclay has written one of the most important books on Paul in recent years, *Paul and the Gift*,[1] and it is the first of a proposed two-volume work.[2] I cannot rehearse the entire book here and so will focus on some elements. The book is divided into four parts: (1) the multiple meanings of "gift," (2) the divine gift in Second Temple Judaism, (3) gift and worth in Galatians, and (4) God's creative gift in Romans.

Gifts in Antiquity and Today

In part 1 Barclay sets forth the various meanings of gift and grace. As readers, says Barclay, we are prone to misunderstand grace and gift since we often define a gift to rule out a reciprocal response or a return of some kind. Those who are the heirs of Immanuel Kant think that gifts should be given without any hope of a return benefit. But in the Greco-Roman world it was expected that one would respond to a gift with some return, and such a return did not mean that the gift was not a true gift. Disinterested altruism did not characterize gifts in the Greco-Roman world. Jacques Derrida, following the train of Kant, maintains that any kind of return nullifies a gift. He thinks a

---

1 John M. G. Barclay, *Paul and the Gift* (Grand Rapids, MI: Eerdmans, 2015).
2 This review was originally published in "*Paul and the Gift*: A Review Article," *Them* 41 (2016): 52–58. It is used by permission. There are a few minor changes to the original review.

pure gift is impossible since a response is always involved. But Barclay notes that Derrida's definition of gift does not accord with how a gift was conceived in the Greco-Roman world. Gifts and reciprocity were not antithetical but complementary, for one was obligated to respond appropriately to a gift. Social bonds were strengthened and formed through both the gift and the response to the gift. Responses to a gift could be expressed in a variety of ways, but one way to respond is with gratitude. In fact, gifts were often given to those who were deemed to be worthy or fitting since to grant gifts to those who were not worthy to receive them was considered to be foolish. It was common to think that one should be discriminating and discerning in giving a gift so that the gift was not wasted on the unworthy. Even Jewish giving to the poor, Barclay argues, fits the paradigm of a return since Jews expected a benefit from God for their generosity.

Definitions of "Gift"

Barclay provides a taxonomy of the meaning of the word "gift." Barclay thinks that gift can be "perfected" (i.e., defined most clearly) six ways:

1. superabundance (the extravagance and scale of the gift);
2. singularity (the giver is always and only benevolent—there is no punishment for evil);
3. priority (the gift is given before there is any initiative on the part of the recipient);
4. incongruity (the gift is given regardless of the worth of the recipient);
5. efficacy (the gift empowers the one to whom it is given); and
6. noncircularity (there is no expected return for the gift).

The notion that gifts are noncircular, as Barclay argues, is a Western notion and was not present in antiquity. We must be careful, Barclay maintains, in using the words "gift" and "grace" since the notion is polyvalent, and one does not necessarily have all six ideas of gift in mind when using the term. Barclay's contribution here is fascinating and enlightening.

History of Interpretation

Barclay considers some notable interpreters of Paul in church history, including Marcion, Augustine, Martin Luther, John Calvin, Karl Barth, and others. I will not comment on everyone Barclay discusses. Marcion's reading of Paul tilts toward *singularity*—God is benevolent so that he loves and saves and delivers instead of judging his creatures. Augustine's understanding of grace is incongruous in that it is given to sinners before they were worthy, but it is also efficacious since the grace given to the ungodly transforms them. As Augustine's thought develops, he emphasizes that grace is prior, efficacious, and incongruous.

Luther, on the other hand, questions the Augustinian understanding of the efficacy of grace as a substance granted to the soul. Like Augustine he features the incongruity of grace—grace is given to those who are ungodly. In fact, Luther's theology stands out since grace remains incongruous for the entirety of one's life.

I dissent from Barclay, however, in his apparent endorsement of the Finnish view of Luther.[3] I think the sources point in another direction as I have argued briefly in my book *Faith Alone*.[4] In any case, Luther teaches the superabundance of grace and its priority, but what stands out in his thought is the incongruity of grace. Barclay also thinks grace in Luther is noncircular since grace is not granted so that we will return it in some fashion—that is, the response of gratitude does not benefit God. The word "benefit" is ambiguous. Luther may have meant that we do not add in any way to God's being and greatness since God is self-sufficient. However, in another sense, gratitude brings God glory. Barclay also says works in Luther are not "integral to faith or to justification."[5] The notion is disputed, however, for as Barclay says, works may have functioned as necessary evidence of

---

3   Barclay, *Paul and the Gift*, 107.
4   Thomas R. Schreiner, *Faith Alone—the Doctrine of Justification: What the Reformers Taught . . . and Why It Still Matters* (Grand Rapids, MI: Zondervan, 2015), 49–52. See also Thomas R. Schreiner, *Justification: An Introduction* (Wheaton, IL: Crossway, 2023), 15–16.
5   Barclay, *Paul and the Gift*, 114.

faith.⁶ In that sense, then, they can be considered as integral to faith and justification in Luther.

In Calvin's theology, according to Barclay, the grace of God is not singular since God also predestines the wicked to damnation. On the other hand, the priority of God's grace in the life of believers is emphasized repeatedly. God's grace, as is the case with Luther, is understood to be incongruous, though Calvin also teaches emphatically that good works follow as a result of God's grace. In Calvin's system, believers are transformed and made holy by the grace of God, and hence grace in Calvin is circular in the sense that there is a return.

E. P. Sanders's covenant nomism focuses on the priority of grace in Second Temple Judaism so that obedience was a response to God's covenant love. Barclay rightly notes, however, a critical mistake in Sanders's work, for Sanders understands the priority of grace as if it also entailed the incongruity of grace. But, says Barclay, it is clear that the rabbis believed grace was given to those who were worthy (in accord with the view of gift in antiquity). Sanders operates as if the Augustinian view of grace were shared by the rabbis. Since he fails to define carefully what grace means, he lumps together priority with incongruity. Sanders rightly dismantled a caricature of Second Temple Judaism, as if grace were nonexistent. At the same time, his insistence on the uniformity of grace was overly simplistic, blinding some scholars to the diversity of ways in which grace was understood in the ancient world.

Barclay takes scholars such as D. A. Carson, Simon Gathercole, and Timo Laato to task for criticizing the notion of grace in Second Temple Judaism. Such criticisms fail, according to Barclay, since various understandings of grace circulated in Second Temple Judaism. Carson, for example, operates as if incongruous grace were the only way to define grace, but other conceptions of grace were present among Jews. Douglas Campbell is also indicted since he assumes that genuine grace precludes the necessity of any human response. Campbell heralds the singularity of grace by saying that God's grace is benevolent while

---

6   Barclay, *Paul and the Gift*, 114n87.

rejecting the notion of God's judgment. Campbell stands out, then, because he sees all six notions of grace in Paul. In this respect, he is closest to Marcion. At the other extreme stands Chris VanLandingham, who makes the mistake of thinking that grace is only incongruous. Thus, since in VanLandingham's scheme obedience is necessary for eternal life, he concludes that grace is lacking in Paul's theology. But this is not necessarily so, warns Barclay, since the notion that grace has no return was not the view of most in the Greco-Roman world. One major conclusion Barclay draws (and it is one of the signal benefits of this work) is that interpreters often disagree because they do not realize that they are operating with different conceptions of grace. Hence, when it comes to Paul and Second Temple Judaism, we are not faced with a stark alternative, says Barclay. They both proclaimed grace. It is not as if Paul believed in grace and Second Temple Judaism denied it. Different Jewish writers mapped out and profiled grace in various ways.

The Gift in Second Temple Judaism

Part 2 of the book considers the divine gift in Second Temple Judaism. Barclay examines The Wisdom of Solomon, Philo of Alexandria, the Qumran Hodayot, Pseudo-Philo's *Liber antiquitatum biblicarum*, and 4 Ezra. I will sum up briefly the conclusions drawn from each author investigated. In Wisdom the superabundance of the gift and God's benevolence come to the forefront. Grace for Wisdom is *congruous* instead of incongruous since the latter would call into question God's wisdom and discernment. Granting gifts to those who waste them is not a mark of goodness for the author of Wisdom. Turning to Philo, we find that in his expositions God's gifts are superabundant and lavish. Philo tends toward singularity in emphasizing God's love and benevolence instead of his justice. God's grace is given to those who are worthy and fitting, but their worth and virtue are not a *cause* for God's grace but only a *condition*. God's grace is prior in the sense that God elects beforehand those who are especially worthy and excellent, for to do otherwise would suggest that God is arbitrary and whimsical. In Philo grace is congruous with the worth of the recipient, but, Barclay notes, such a view did not mean in antiquity that Philo did not believe in grace. As he has already demonstrated, gifts and the worthiness of the recipient were a common theme in the ancient world.

The Qumran Hoyadot proclaim the abundance and lavishness of God's grace, but what is most striking is the incongruity of grace since the writer often confesses his worthlessness and shame. In this respect, he is quite similar to Paul. The efficacy of God's grace also is a hallmark of the hymns. Barclay observes that both Philo and Wisdom would have rejected the incongruity of grace proclaimed in the Hoyadot. We see plainly that grace was not parsed in the same way by every Second Temple Jew. Barclay adds that we should not say one form of grace is purer or higher; instead, we should recognize that grace is defined and understood differently by various Jewish writers. Sanders's attempt to lump virtually all of Second Temple Jews under the rubric of covenant nomism does not do justice to the complexity of the evidence and to the various conceptions of grace that were circulating.

Pseudo-Philo's *Liber antiquitatum biblicarum*, like the Hoyadot, reflects an emphasis on the incongruity of grace. In fact, no book in Second Temple Judaism emphasizes God's mercy as much as this one, for God will keep his covenant promises to his people, even after they sin and experience divine judgment. God's grace is incongruous toward Israel because they are his elect people. Fourth Ezra moves in another direction. God's mercy is reserved for the righteous who keep God's commands. Barclay says we should not label such as works righteousness since in doing so we reflect Protestant and Augustinian views that true grace is incongruous.

Barclay remarks that all of these Second Temple works emphasize the superabundance of God's grace. At the same time, none of them define grace in terms of noncircularity—some return for grace is expected, even if that return is thanksgiving (this makes me wonder, as noted above, why Barclay thinks Luther's notion of thanksgiving does not reflect circularity). Only Philo tends toward the singularity of grace. Some writers stress the priority and efficacy of God's grace, but the major difference emerges on the incongruity of grace, which is celebrated by Pseudo-Philo and Hoyadot and denied by Wisdom of Solomon, Philo, and 4 Ezra. Many in antiquity believed that God's gifts should be given to the fitting, to those who are worthy. Hence, says Barclay, we should not say that those who hold to congruous grace deny grace; they just espoused a different notion of grace. Barclay rightly adjusts Sanders's work, showing that there is more to say about grace than its priority. Sanders was on target in saying that grace was prior but failed to see that there were other dimensions of grace, and hence it is not sufficient to lump all Second Temple Jews together as if they held to the same theology of grace. What stands out is that some Second Temple Jewish writers think grace is congruous, while others think it is incongruous.

Once we see the diversity of grace in Jewish thought, says Barclay, "it becomes senseless to ask whether Paul represents 'real' grace, as opposed to its 'diluted' forms in Judaism."[7] He also says about Paul, "It would make little sense to say that he emphasizes grace *more* than other Jews of his time, but it is also clear that his views are not identical to those of the others surveyed, just as they disagree among themselves."[8] Scholars indebted to the Reformation criticized Sanders when they detected congruous grace, thinking they had shown that grace was not present where it was conditioned. But, says Barclay, such a notion misfires if we recognize that grace was understood in multiple ways.

Some Reflections on Barclay's Contribution in Parts 1 and 2

Barclay's work represents a significant advance in qualifying and correcting Sanders's monolithic reading of Second Temple Judaism, though others have gone before him. We can think of a number of works here: the first volume of *Justification and Variegated Nomism*, Simon Gathercole's *Where Is Boasting?*, Mark Elliott's *The Survivors of Israel*, and Andrew Das's *Paul, the Law, and the Covenant*.[9] Barclay

---

7   Barclay, *Paul and the Gift*, 320.
8   Barclay, *Paul and the Gift*, 328.
9   D. A. Carson, Peter T. O'Brien, and Mark A. Seifrid, eds., *The Complexities of Second Temple Judaism*, vol. 1 of *Justification and Variegated Nomism* (Grand Rapids, MI: Baker, 2001);

also distinguishes himself from other scholars in saying that we cannot say that there is purer or higher or better grace in Paul. The incongruous grace of Paul is not superior to the congruous conception of grace in Wisdom of Solomon. Grace is still grace; it is just a different kind of grace. Barclay helpfully delineates that the dispute between Paul and other Jews of his day was due, at least in part, to different conceptions of grace.

Barclay approaches the matter descriptively and historically and thus concludes that each writer's depiction of gift and grace should be appreciated for what it is. Fair enough. His historical work is invaluable and helps us demarcate more carefully how Paul stands over against other contemporaries. We get a much sharper profile from Barclay than we did from Sanders. At the same time, Barclay brackets out in advance another standpoint—one that is at least implicitly at work in Carson and others. Let me put it straightforwardly. For those who think that Paul's writings are the inspired word of God, the Pauline conception of grace is superior to construals of grace that depart from his understanding. Obviously, there is not space to defend what I am suggesting. Still, it is questionable to think that a strictly historical framework is to be preferred over a theological stance that accepts Paul's theology as the word of God. Most recognize that there is no neutral place to stand in doing history or exegesis. Of course, that does not mean that our philosophical starting point is arbitrary. If Paul and Wisdom of Solomon disagree on the nature of grace, we (as Protestants) follow Paul instead of Wisdom. Wisdom propounds a particular theology of grace, but Paul rejects Wisdom's construal of grace, and as believers we confess and believe that Paul's theology of grace is superior to what we find in Wisdom or Philo.

If we consider history, the matter being disputed here is hardly new. No knowledgeable Protestant denies, for instance, that Roman

---

Simon J. Gathercole, *Where Is Boasting? Early Jewish Soteriology and Paul's Response in Romans 1–5* (Grand Rapids, MI: Eerdmans, 2002); Mark A. Elliott, *The Survivors of Israel: A Reconsideration of the Theology of Pre-Christian Judaism* (Grand Rapids, MI: Eerdmans, 2000); Andrew A. Das, *Paul, the Law, and the Covenant* (Peabody, MA: Hendrickson, 2001).

Catholics believe in grace. The problem is that the Roman Catholic definition of grace, according to Protestants, does not conform to the biblical witness, and hence the Roman Catholic conception of grace is judged to be substandard. I am grateful for Barclay's clear delineation of the various conceptions of grace and for his recognition of various strands in Second Temple sources. The typology he uses represents a helpful advance and clarification. On the other hand, his work does not change the landscape dramatically. Others (including the Reformers) recognized, even if they did not use the same terminology, that there were different conceptions of grace in Second Temple sources and between Roman Catholics and Protestants. Barclay helps us see that all players in Second Temple Judaism believed in grace, even if they understood it differently. But it does not follow from this that we should accept all conceptions of grace as equally valid, for that is a theological question that cannot and should not be decided by history.

Gift in Galatians

In parts 3 and 4, Barclay studies both Galatians and Romans. For the sake of this review I will limit myself to a few observations since there is much to appreciate exegetically and theologically, but there is not space to comment on every insight. Barclay focuses in Galatians on the new communities Paul wants to form with his gospel, emphasizing the incongruity of the gift in Paul. God's grace is granted to the unworthy and the undeserving. What Paul says accords in part with Hoyadot and Pseudo-Philo, but by way of contrast Paul celebrates the grace of God given in Jesus Christ.

Barclay argues in Galatians that "works of the law" refers to the entire torah but that we should not conclude that the Pauline rejection of works of the law signals a defective soteriology on the part of the opponents. If Paul were waging war against works righteousness, says Barclay, he would not speak negatively of uncircumcision as well (Gal 5:6; 6:15). The problem is not that believers can't keep the law, according to Barclay. Instead, the torah is not normative for believers any longer; the new community is not demarcated by the torah.

I am not persuaded that there is no polemic against works righteousness in Galatians. Faith is set against doing, even if the doing is circumscribed by torah (Gal. 3:1–9). The contrast is particularly strong in Galatians 3:12 where the law, in contrast to faith, is characterized by performance. The reference to uncircumcision does not negate the point being made here since people may boast in what they do (get circumcised) or what they do not do (uncircumcision), which explains why Paul trumpets the cross as his only boast (Gal. 6:12) and the new creation as the rule by which all should live (6:15–16). Additionally, Barclay does not reflect enough on the difference between promise and law. Law does not avail since it focuses on what human beings do (or, more precisely, fail to do), while the promise stresses what God in Christ does for believers. Of course, this last point fits with Barclay's emphasis on the incongruity of grace in Galatians, and he rightly features that theme. He also correctly says that we see both the incongruity and congruity of grace in the letter; it is incongruous since it is given to the unworthy, but it is also congruous in that it fits and shapes believers so that they are transformed and become worthy. Barclay does not see much evidence of the efficacy of grace in Galatians, but I wonder if his own work on the transforming power of the Spirit points in the other direction.

Gift in Romans

When it comes to Romans, Barclay sees a pronounced emphasis on the superabundance of grace. In Romans, like Galatians, Paul sees God's grace as incongruous, in that it is granted to the unworthy, and fitting, in that it changes those who are its recipients. The incongruous grace of God continues to be given in Jesus Christ. At the final judgment there will be evidence that those who have received God's grace have changed. Hence, God's grace is unconditioned (given to the unworthy), but not unconditional (those who have received such grace are transformed). Barclay helpfully maintains that the discussion of Abraham in Romans 4 engages in a polemic against works *and* emphasizes the inclusion of the Gentiles; there is no reason to opt for an either–or.

Paul's inclusion of the Gentiles and his Gentile mission accords with his theology of grace.

On the other hand, Barclay is not convincing when he says that there is no polemic against a Jewish conception of works in Romans 4:4–5. Has not Barclay already shown that some would not agree with Paul's notion of an incongruous gift? In these verses we see a different conception of grace. Some Jews certainly depended on their works for vindication; otherwise, the boasting of the Pharisee in the parable of the Pharisee and tax collector (Luke 18:9–14) does not relate to anyone. Barclay thinks Paul has an exegetical but not a polemical purpose in Romans 4:4–5, but that is a very unlikely splitting of categories. Paul doesn't write in abstract theological categories but addresses existential and real struggles in the lives of human beings.

In the same way, it seems as if Barclay strains to deny any sense of trusting in one's own righteousness in Romans 9:30–10:8. In Barclay's reading of Romans 10:3, Paul speaks of confirming or validating one's righteousness instead of establishing or achieving righteousness. According to Barclay, Paul doesn't criticize an attempt to be righteous by works or human achievement. The issue is that some believed that torah observance made one a fitting recipient of God's kindness. Paul does not criticize works righteousness "but the criteria by which worth is defined."[10] This is a possible reading, but it is a very fine distinction. It seems likely that people would boast about meeting such criteria. Indeed, Paul sets boasting and works over against faith in Romans 3:27–4:5.

Surprisingly (at least to me), Barclay argues that the post-Pauline writers of Ephesians (2:8–10), 2 Timothy (1:9), and Titus (3:5) indict "pride of achievement" where there is "the human tendency to self-congratulation in the *attainment* of worth."[11] So, according to Barclay, the post-Pauline writers actually subscribe to a view of works and faith that most Protestants have thought was in Romans and Galatians. I think all these later letters are authentically Pauline, but let us

10 Barclay, *Paul and the Gift*, 541n46.
11 Barclay, *Paul and the Gift*, 571 (italics in original).

follow Barclay's argument a bit further. Presumably these post-Pauline writers were interpreting Romans and Galatians for their generation. I would suggest that we should follow their interpretation (if they are post-Pauline) instead of Barclay's. They were closer to Paul in time and culture than Barclay, and they understood Paul to criticize works righteousness. Of course, if these letters are Pauline (as I think they are), they constitute further evidence for the notion that Paul engaged in a polemic against works righteousness.

Conclusion

I have probably concentrated too much on places where I disagree with Barclay. His study of "gift" in antiquity is of great value. Barclay demonstrates clearly that grace and gift were conceived of in a diversity of ways in Second Temple Judaism. All Jews in the Second Temple period believed in grace, but they conceived of it in various ways, and thus Barclay's work represents a real advance over Sanders's construal. Barclay also demonstrates that one of the goals of Paul's ministry was the unification of Jews and Gentiles in the church, and Paul's theology of the gift was the basis for this new community. The incongruity of God's gift of grace stands out in Paul, and Paul emphasizes that the gift is given in the Christ event. Finally, the book is full of profound and thought-provoking exegetical insights, and hence this book is sure to be discussed for years to come.

Recommended Resources

Commentaries

Betz, H. D. *Galatians: A Commentary on Paul's Letter to the Churches in Galatia*. Hermeneia. Philadelphia: Fortress, 1979.

Bruce, F. F. *The Epistle to the Galatians: A Commentary on the Greek Text*. NIGTC. Grand Rapids, MI: Eerdmans, 1982.

Calvin, John. *Galatians, Ephesians, Philippians and Colossians*. Translated by T. H. L. Parker. Edited by David W. Torrance and Thomas F. Torrance. Calvin's New Testament Commentaries 11. Grand Rapids, MI: Eerdmans, 1965.

Das, A. Andrew. *Galatians*. ConcC. St. Louis: Concordia, 2014.

De Boer, Martinus. *Galatians*. NTL. Louisville: Westminster John Knox, 2011.

Dunn, James D. G. *The Epistle to the Galatians*. BNTC. Peabody, MA: Hendrickson, 1993.

Esler, Philip F. *Galatians*. New York: Routledge, 1998.

Fee, Gordon D. *Galatians*. Pentecostal Commentary. Dorset, UK: Deo, 2007.

George, Timothy. *Galatians*. CSC. 2nd ed. Nashville: Holman Reference, 2020.

Hansen, G. Walter. *Galatians*. IVPNTC. Downers Grove, IL: InterVarsity, 1994.

Hays, Richard B. *The Letter to the Galatians: Introduction, Commentary, and Reflections*. Pages 181–348 in vol. 11 of *The New Interpreter's Bible*. Nashville: Abingdon, 2000.

Keener, Craig S. *Galatians*. Grand Rapids, MI: Eerdmans, 2019.
Lightfoot, J. B. *The Epistle of St. Paul to the Galatians with Introductions, Notes and Dissertations*. Reprint. Grand Rapids, MI: Zondervan, 1957.
Longenecker, Richard N. *Galatians*. WBC. Dallas: Word, 1990.
Lührmann, Dieter. *Galatians*. CC. Translated by O. C. Dean Jr. Minneapolis: Fortress, 1992.
Luther, Martin. *Lectures on Galatians 1535: Chapters 1–4*. Vol. 26 of *Luther's Works*. Edited by Jarislov Pelikan. St. Louis: Concordia, 1963.
Luther, Martin. *Lectures on Galatians, 1535: Chapters 5–6. Lectures on Galatians 1519: Chapters 1–6*. Vol. 27 of *Luther's Works*. Edited by Jarislov Pelikan. St. Louis: Concordia, 1963.
Martyn, J. Louis. *Galatians: A New Translation with Introduction and Commentary*. AB. New York: Doubleday, 1997.
Matera, Frank J. *Galatians*. SP. Collegeville, MN: Liturgical Press, 1992.
McKnight, Scot. *Galatians*. NIVAC. Grand Rapids, MI: Zondervan, 1995.
Moo, Douglas J. *Galatians*. BECNT. Grand Rapids, MI: Baker Academic, 2013.
Oakes, Peter. *Galatians*. Paideia Commentaries on the New Testament. Grand Rapids, MI: Baker Academic, 2015.
Schreiner, Thomas R. *Galatians*. ZECNT. Grand Rapids, MI: Zondervan, 2010.
Silva, Moisés. "Galatians." Pages 785–812 in *Commentary on the New Testament Use of the Old Testament*. Edited by G. K. Beale and D. A. Carson. Grand Rapids, MI: Baker, 2007.
Williams, Jarvis J. *Galatians*. NCC. Eugene, OR: Cascade, 2020.
Witherington, Ben, III. *Grace in Galatia: A Commentary on Paul's Letter to the Galatians*. Grand Rapids, MI: Eerdmans, 1998.

Monographs

Barclay, John M. G. *Obeying the Truth: Paul's Ethics in Galatians*. Minneapolis: Fortress, 1988.
Barclay, John M. G. *Paul and the Gift*. Grand Rapids, MI: Eerdmans, 2015.

Bird, Michael F. *The Saving Righteousness of God: Studies on Paul, Justification, and the New Perspective*. Eugene, OR: Wipf & Stock, 2007.

Burke, Trevor J. *Adoption into God's Family: Exploring a Pauline Metaphor*. NSBT 22. Downers Grove, IL: InterVarsity, 2006.

Carson, D. A., Peter T. O'Brien, and Mark A. Seifrid, eds. *The Complexities of Second Temple Judaism*. Vol. 1 of *Justification and Variegated Nomism*. Grand Rapids, MI: Baker, 2001.

Carson, D. A., Peter T. O'Brien, and Mark A. Seifrid, eds. *The Paradoxes of Paul*. Vol. 2 of *Justification and Variegated Nomism*. Grand Rapids, MI: Baker, 2004.

Ciampa, Roy E. *The Presence and Function of Scripture in Galatians 1 and 2*. WUNT 2/102. Tübingen: Mohr Siebeck, 1998.

Das, A. Andrew. *Paul, the Law, and the Covenant*. Peabody, MA: Hendrickson, 2001.

Dunn, James D. G. *The New Perspective on Paul: Collected Essays*. WUNT 185. Tübingen: Mohr Siebeck, 2005.

Eastman, Susan G. *Recovering Paul's Mother Tongue: Language and Theology in Galatians*. Grand Rapids, MI: Eerdmans, 2007.

Elliott, Mark A. *The Survivors of Israel: A Reconsideration of the Theology of Pre-Christian Judaism*. Grand Rapids, MI: Eerdmans, 2000.

Elliott, Mark W., Scott J. Hafemann, N. T. Wright, and John Frederick. *Galatians and Christian Theology: Justification, the Gospel, and Ethics in Paul's Letter*. Grand Rapids, MI: Baker, 2014.

Elliott, Susan. *Cutting Too Close for Comfort: Paul's Letter to the Galatians in Its Anatolian Cultic Context*. JSNTSup 248. London: T&T Clark, 2003.

Gathercole, Simon J. *Where Is Boasting? Early Jewish Soteriology and Paul's Response in Romans 1–5*. Grand Rapids, MI: Eerdmans, 2002.

Hansen, G. Walter. *Abraham in Galatians: Epistolary and Rhetorical Contexts*. JSNTSup 29. Sheffield: Sheffield Academic Press, 1989.

Hardin, Justin K. *Galatians and the Imperial Cult: A Critical Analysis of the First-Century Social Context of Paul's Letter*. WUNT 2/237. Tübingen: Mohr Siebeck, 2008.

Harmon, Matthew S. *She Must and Shall Go Free: Paul's Isaianic Gospel in Galatians*. BZNW 168. Berlin: De Gruyter, 2010.

Hays, Richard B. *The Faith of Jesus Christ: An Investigation of the Narrative Substructure of Galatians 3:1–4:11*. 2nd ed. Grand Rapids, MI: Eerdmans, 2002.

Hong, In-Gyu. *The Law in Galatians*. JSNTSup 81. Sheffield: Sheffield Academic Press, 1993.

Hove, Richard W. *Equality in Christ? Galatians 3:28 and the Gender Dispute*. Wheaton, IL: Crossway, 1999.

Kern, Philip H. *Rhetoric in Galatians: Assessing an Approach to Paul's Epistle*. SNTSMS 101. Cambridge: Cambridge University Press, 1998.

Kim, Seyoon. *Paul and the New Perspective: Second Thoughts on the Origin of Paul's Gospel*. Grand Rapids, MI: Eerdmans, 2002.

Luther, Martin. *The Freedom of a Christian: A New Translation*. Translated by Robert Kolb. Crossway Short Classics. Wheaton, IL: Crossway, 2023.

McFadden, Kevin. *Faith in the Son of God: The Place of Christ-Oriented Faith within Pauline Theology*. Wheaton, IL: Crossway, 2021.

Schreiner, Thomas R. *Faith Alone—the Doctrine of Justification: What the Reformers Taught . . . and Why It Still Matters*. Grand Rapids, MI: Zondervan, 2015.

Schreiner, Thomas R. *Justification: An Introduction*. SSST. Wheaton, IL: Crossway, 2023.

Silva, Moisés. *Interpreting Galatians: Explorations in Exegetical Method*. 2nd ed. Grand Rapids, MI: Baker Academic, 2001.

Sprinkle, Preston. *Law and Life: The Interpretation of Leviticus 18:5 in Early Judaism and Paul*. WUNT 2/241. Tübingen: Mohr Siebeck, 2008.

Westerholm, Stephen. *Perspectives Old and New on Paul: The "Lutheran" Paul and His Critics*. Grand Rapids, MI: Eerdmans, 2004.

Williams, Jarvis J. *Christ Redeemed "Us" from the Curse of the Law: A Jewish Martyrological Reading of Galatians 3.13*. LNTS 524. New York: T&T Clark, 2019.

Williams, Jarvis J. *The Spirit, Ethics, and Eternal Life: Paul's Vision for the Christian Life in Galatians*. Downers Grove, IL: IVP Academic, 2023.

Wilson, Todd A. *The Curse of the Law and the Crisis in Galatia: Reassessing the Purpose of Galatians*. WUNT 2/225. Tübingen: Mohr Siebeck, 2007.

Articles and Essays

Arnold, Clinton. "Returning to the Domain of the Powers: *Stoicheia* as Evil Spirits in Galatians 4:3, 9." *NovT* 38 (1996): 55–76.

Barclay, John M. G. "Mirror-Reading a Polemical Letter: Galatians as a Test Case." *JSNT* 31 (1987): 73–93.

Barrett, C. K. "The Allegory of Abraham, Sarah, and Hagar in the Argument of Galatians." Pages 1–16 in *Rechtfertigung: Festschrift für Ernest Käsemann*. Edited by J. Friedrich, W. Pöhlmann, and P. Stuhlmacher. Tübingen: Mohr Siebeck, 1976.

Beale, G. K. "Peace and Mercy upon the Israel of God. The Old Testament Background of Galatians 6:16b." *Bib* 80 (1999): 204–23.

Betz, H. D. "The Literary Composition and Function of Paul's Letter to the Galatians." *NTS* 21 (1975): 352–79.

Carson, D. A. "Pauline Inconsistency: Reflections on 1 Corinthians 9:19–23 and Galatians 2:11–14." *Churchman* 100 (1986), 6–45.

Carson, D. A. "The Vindication of Imputation: On Fields of Discourse and Semantic Fields." Pages 46–78 in *Justification: What's at Stake in Current Debates*. Edited by Mark Husbands and Daniel J. Treier. Downers Grove, IL: InterVarsity, 2004.

Cohn-Sherbok, Dan. "Some Reflections on James Dunn's 'The Incident at Antioch (Gal 2:11–18).' " *JSNT* 18 (1983): 68–74.

Collins, C. John. "Galatians 3:16: What Kind of Exegete Was Paul?" *TynB* 54 (2003): 75–86.

Collins, C. John. "A Syntactical Note (Genesis 3:15): Is the Woman's Seed Singular or Plural?" *TynB* 48 (1997): 139–48.

Davis, Anne. "Allegorically Speaking in Galatians 4:21–5:1." *BBR* 14 (2004): 161–74.

De Boer, Martinus. "The Meaning of the Phrase *ta stoicheia tou kosmou* in Galatians." *NTS* 53 (2007): 204–24.

De Boer, Martinus. "Paul's Quotation of Isaiah 54.1 in Galatians 4.27." *NTS* 50 (2004): 370–89.

De Boer, Martinus. "Paul's Use and Interpretation of a Justification Tradition in Galatians 2.15–21." *JSNT* 28 (2005): 189–216.

Dunn, James D. G. "The Incident at Antioch (Gal 2:11–18)." *JSNT* 18 (1983): 3–57.

Dunn, James D. G. "The New Perspective on Paul." *BJRL* 65 (1983) 95–122.

Dunn, James D. G. "Works of the Law and the Curse of the Law (Galatians 3:10–14)." *NTS* 31 (1985): 523–42.

Dunn, James D. G. "Yet Once More—'The Works of the Law': A Response." *JSNT* 46 (1992): 99–117.

Eastman, Susan G. "'Cast Out the Slave Woman and Her Son': The Dynamics of Exclusion and Inclusion in Galatians 4.30." *JSNT* 28 (2006): 309–36.

Eastman, Susan G. "The Evil Eye and the Curse of the Law: Galatians 3.1 Revisited." *JSNT* 83 (2001): 69–87.

Fitzmyer, Joseph A. "Crucifixion in Ancient Palestine, Qumran Literature, and the New Testament." *CBQ* 40 (1978): 493–513.

Fitzmyer, Joseph A. "Paul's Jewish Background and the Deeds of the Law." Pages 18–35 in *According to Paul: Studies in the Theology of the Apostle*. New York: Paulist, 1993.

Gathercole, Simon J. "Torah, Life, and Salvation: Leviticus 18:5 in Early Judaism and the New Testament." Pages 131–50 in *From Prophecy to Testament: The Function of the Old Testament in the New*. Edited by C. A. Evans and J. A. Sanders. Peabody, MA: Hendrickson, 2004.

Grindheim, Sigurd. "Apostate Turned Prophet: Paul's Prophetic Understanding and Prophetic Hermeneutic with Special Reference to Galatians 3.10–12." *NTS* 53 (2007): 545–65.

Gundry, Robert H. "Grace, Works, and Staying Saved in Paul." *Bib* 66 (1985): 1–38.

Harrisville, Roy A., III, "Before ΠΙΣΤΙΣ ΧΡΙΣΤΟΥ: The Objective Genitive as Good Greek." *NovT* 41 (2006): 353–58.

Hays, Richard B. "Christology and Ethics in Galatians: The Law of Christ." *CBQ* 49 (1987): 268–90.

Hong, In-Gyu. "Does Paul Misrepresent the Jewish Law? Law and Covenant in Gal 3:1–14." *NovT* 36 (1994): 164–82.

Houlden, J. L. "A Response to James D. G. Dunn." *JSNT* 18 (1983): 58–67.

Hughes, John J. "Hebrews IX 15ff. and Galatians III 15ff.: A Study in Covenant Practice and Procedure." *NovT* 21 (1979): 27–96.

Hunn, Debbie. "The Baptism of Galatians 3:27: A Contextual Approach." *ExpTim* 115 (2005): 372–75.

Hunn, Debbie. "Debating the Faithfulness of Jesus Christ in Twentieth-Century Scholarship." Pages 15–31 in *The Faith of Jesus Christ: Exegetical, Biblical, and Theological Studies*. Edited by Michael F. Bird and Preston Sprinkle. Peabody, MA: Hendrickson, 2009.

Hunn, Debbie. "*Ean mē* in Galatians 2:16: A Look at Greek Literature." *NovT* 49 (2007): 281–90.

Jewett, Robert. "The Agitators and the Galatian Congregation." Pages 334–47 in *The Galatians Debate: Contemporary Issues in Rhetorical and Historical Interpretation*. Edited by Mark D. Nanos. Peabody, MA: Hendrickson, 2002.

Jobes, Karen H. "Jerusalem, Our Mother: Metalepsis and Intertextuality in Galatians 4:21–31." *WTJ* 55 (1993): 299–320.

Johnson, S. Lewis, Jr. "Paul and 'the Israel of God': An Exegetical and Eschatological Case-Study." Pages 181–96 in *Essays in Honor of J. Dwight Pentecost*. Edited by Stanley D. Touissaint and Charles H. Dyer. Chicago: Moody, 1986.

Köstenberger, Andreas. "The Identity of the *Israēl tou theou* (Israel of God) in Galatians 6:16." *Faith and Mission* 19 (2001): 3–24.

Longenecker, Bruce W. "'Until Christ Is Formed in You': Suprahuman Forces and Moral Character in Galatians." *CBQ* 61 (1999): 92–108.

Longenecker, Richard N. "The Pedagogical Nature of the Law in Galatians 3:19–4:7." *JETS* 25 (1982): 53–61.

Lull, D. J. "'The Law Was Our Pedagogue': A Study in Galatians 3.19–25." *JBL* 105 (1986): 481–98.

Martyn, J. Louis. "Apocalyptic Antinomies in Paul's Letter to the Galatians." *NTS* 31 (1985): 410–24.

Matlock, R. Barry. "Detheologizing the *PISTIS CRISTOU* Debate: Cautionary Remarks from a Lexical Semantic Perspective." *NovT* 42 (2000): 1–23.

Matlock, R. Barry. "'Even the Demons Believe': Paul and *Pistis Christou*." *CBQ* 64 (2002): 300–318.

Matlock, R. Barry. "*PISTIS* in Galatians 3:26: Neglected Evidence for 'Faith in Christ'?" *NTS* 49 (2003): 433–39.

Matlock, R. Barry. "Saving Faith: The Rhetoric and Semantics of *Pistis* in Paul." Pages 73–89 in *The Faith of Jesus Christ: Exegetical, Biblical, and Theological Studies*. Edited by Michael F. Bird and Preston Sprinkle. Peabody, MA: Hendrickson, 2009.

Moo, Douglas J. "'Law,' 'Works of the Law,' and Legalism in Paul." *WTJ* 45 (1983): 73–100.

Porter, Stanley E., and Andrew W. Pitts. "*Pistis* with a Preposition and Genitive Modifier: Lexical, Semantic and Syntactic Considerations in the *Pistis Christou* Discussion." Pages 33–53 in *The Faith of Jesus Christ: Exegetical, Biblical, and Theological Studies*. Edited by Michael F. Bird and Preston Sprinkle. Peabody: Hendrickson, 2009.

Schreiner, Thomas R. "'Works of Law' in Paul." *NovT* 33 (1991): 217–44.

Schreiner, Thomas R. "Paul, Luther, and Justification in Gal 2:15–21." *WTJ* 65 (2003): 215–230.

Silva, Moisés, "Faith versus Works of Law in Galatians." Pages 217–48 in *The Paradoxes of Paul*. Vol. 2 of *Justification and Variegated Nomism*. Edited by D. A. Carson, P. T. O'Brien, and M. A. Seifrid. Grand Rapids, MI: Baker, 2004.

Weima, Jeffrey A. D. "Gal 6:11–18: A Hermeneutical Key to the Galatian Letter." *CTJ* 28 (1993): 90–107.

General Index

Abraham, 41, 62, 67–68, 80, 97–109, 124, 134
Abrahamic covenant, 85–86
abundance, 130
Adam, 36, 112
adoption, 42, 55, 72
adultery, 39, 82, 89, 90
adversaries, 3–13
age to come, 34
agitators, 49, 108, 124
alienation, 114
allegory, 98
already-but-not-yet eschatology, 36
anathema, 16
anger, 114
animal sacrifices, 80–81
anthropology, 66
antimony, 42–43
antinomianism, 124
Antioch, 78, 103–6, 109
Antiochus IV Epiphanes, 9
apocalypse, 32, 33, 45, 54, 66, 123
apostles, 5, 27, 50
atonement, 53–54
Augustine, 127, 128, 130
authority, 27

Babylonian exile, 52
babysitters, 87
baptism, 101
Barclay, John, 117, 125–36
Barnabas, 7, 23, 24, 25, 103, 105
Barth, Karl, 127

bear one another's burdens, 117, 119
Beker, J. C., 31–32n2
believers, 51, 68, 87, 101, 108
biting words, 116
bitterness, 114
boasting, 118
boundary markers, 81, 82
Burke, Trevor, 55

calling, 122
Calvin, John, 127, 128
Campbell, Douglas, 128–29
Canaan, 39
Carson, D. A., 128, 132
Chalcedonian Christology, 55
Christian life, 112, 115
Christology, 98, 100
Christus Victor, 53
church
    of Jesus Christ, 99–100
    life in, 117
    "pillars" of, 24
    provision of, 121
    unity of, 107, 108–9
circumcision
    adversaries on, 4, 5
    as covenant sign, 8
    and the cross, 47–56, 123–24
    demanded observance of, 6–12
    as limited to males, 101
    as matter of indifference, 35
    as no longer required, 33, 85
community life, 103

conceit, 116, 117
congruity, 134
consummation, 32
contextualization, 26n11
conviction, 25, 26
Cornelius, 104
corporate responsibility, 116–19
corruption, 120
covenant
  breaking of, 12, 39
  promises of, 31, 58, 86
  and righteousness, 58
  sign of, 8, 9, 11
  temporary nature of, 85–88
covenant faithfulness, 58
covenant membership, 57, 64, 100
covenant nomism, 76, 128
covetousness, 89
Craigie, Peter, 53
credentials, 50
creeds, 55
critical words, 116
cross
  centrality of, 51, 70
  and circumcision, 47–56, 123–24
  and grace, 56
  meaning of, 50–56
culture, 102–3, 136
curse, 16–17, 52–53, 72, 79, 83

Damascus road, 17, 21, 22, 27
damnation, 128
Das, Andrew, 131
David, 80
day of judgment, 44, 45, 60–61, 119, 120, 134
death, 35, 50
deliverance, 72
Demas, 34
Derrida, Jacques, 125–26
dietary requirements, 103
disobedience, 52, 61
dissension, 114
divine sovereignty, 118
drunkenness, 114
Dunn, James, 77–78

ecclesiology, 57
efficacy, 126, 130
Elihu, 59
Elijah, 19
Elliott, Mark, 131
Enlightenment, 16
equality, 101
eschatological reward, 120
eschatological spirit, 36–39
eschatology, 32, 36, 43–44, 45, 118, 123
eternal life, 64, 120, 129
ethnic background, 102, 124
ethnicity, 43
ethnocentrism, 78, 79
exagorazō, 52
exegesis, 132
exile, 38–39, 52
exodus, 52, 71
Ezra, 40

faith
  of Abraham, 67–68
  and death, 51
  as instrument of salvation, 73
  in Jesus Christ, 61, 66, 69, 100, 108, 124
  justification by, 43–44
  vs. the law, 64–69, 134
  object of, 65
false brothers, 7, 23, 26, 27, 42, 106
false teachers, 118
family of Abraham, 97–109, 124
fear, 25
femaleness, 101
Festus, 18
fighting, 114
final judgment. *See* day of judgment, 120
final justification, 44
financial assistance, 119–21
Finnish view, of Luther, 127
flesh, 37, 111, 112
food laws, 78, 103, 104
forensic justification, 58–63
forgiveness, 54
freedom, 39–43, 45, 52, 55, 72, 102, 111

friendship, 108
fruit of the Spirit, 90, 113–15, 121
"fullness of time," 41, 54, 72

Gathercole, Simon, 128, 131
gender, 43, 124
generosity, 119–21, 126
Gentiles, 24, 25, 26, 43, 78, 98, 99, 102, 103, 135
gift
   in antiquity and today, 125–26
   definitions of, 126
   in Galatians, 133–34
   in Romans, 134–36
   in Second Temple Judaism, 129–31
God
   character, 91
   grace of, 57, 62
   as judge, 60
   mercy of, 130
   promises of, 32, 62
   providence of, 4
   sovereignty of, 113
good works, 128
gospel
   denial of, 106
   equal partners in, 24
   as independent, 16–22
   and law of Christ, 93
   of Paul, 6, 27, 123
   as ratified, 22–27
   social implications of, 103–8, 109
   truth of, 3, 17, 23, 27, 42, 51, 105, 107, 108, 124
   unity of, 109
gossip, 114
grace
   and the cross, 56
   history of interpretation of, 127–29
   vs. law, 88, 111
   meanings of, 125–26
   Roman Catholics on, 132–33
   See also gift
gratitude, 126, 127
Greco-Roman world, 125, 126, 129
Greek grammar, 65, 99

Hagar, 84
Hasmoneans, 40
hatred, 114
heart of flesh, 39
heart of stone, 39
heavenly Jerusalem, 35–36
Herod Agrippa II, 18
Herod the Great, 40
history, 132
Holy Spirit
   direction of, 83–84
   fruit of, 90
   generosity by, 119–21
   gift of, 36, 38, 88
   life in, 111–22
   marching in step with, 115–16
   outpouring of, 38, 45
   power of, 90, 91, 92, 112–13, 121
   promise of, 68
   responsibility in, 116–19
   transformation of, 124, 134
   work of, 63
homosexuality, 102
hope, 44
human autonomy, 16, 115
human fallenness, 52
human flourishing, 91
human nature, 83
human responsibility, 118
husbands, 102, 114
hyper-Calvinism, 66
hypocrisy, 26

idolatry, 49, 82, 113
imperative, 116
inclusio, 34, 49
incongruity, 126, 128, 129, 130, 134, 135
indicative, 116
individual piety, 117
individual responsibility, 116–19
influence, 49
Isaiah, 21
Ishmael, 84, 98
Israel of God, 98–100
Izates of Adiabene (King), 10

James, 23, 24, 25, 26, 105
jealousy, 114
Jeremiah, 21
Jerusalem, 4, 35–36
Jesus Christ
  becoming a curse for us, 72
  cross of, 15, 50
  death of, 42, 47, 48, 51
  deity of, 54
  faithfulness of, 64–65, 66–67
  fulfillment of, 86
  full humanity of, 54–55
  law of, 92, 93
  as Messiah, 6, 20, 44
  obedience of, 55, 67
  resurrection of, 33, 34, 37, 61, 70, 71
  sacrifice of, 73
John, 23, 24, 26
Josephus, 10
Joshua, 39
joy, 115
Judaism
  conversion to, 11
  vs. Gentiles, 78
  and the law, 18
  of Paul, 20
  resurrection in, 32–33
judgment, 83
justice, 59, 129
justification
  basis of, 70–73
  as eschatological, 43–44
  as forensic, 58–63
  and righteousness, 57
  as soteriological, 63–64

Kant, Immanuel, 125
kindness, 115
kinship, 100

Laato, Timo, 128
law
  and death, 50–51
  demanded observance of, 6–12, 48
  vs. faith, 64–69
  fulfillment of, 86, 89–93
  and grace, 56
  as guardian, 87
  inadequacy of, 84
  justification through, 68, 75–85
  of love, 92
  obedience to, 18, 71, 79
  promotion of, 124
  and sin, 82–83
  works of, 61, 75–76, 78–79
lawlessness, 93
leadership, 102
legalism, 76, 77
Lewis, C. S., 117
liberation, 72
liberty, 16
licentiousness, 111, 124
love, 90, 92, 114–15
Luther, Martin, 127–28
lying, 39

maleness, 101
Marcion, 127, 129
Martyn, J. Louis, 31–32n2, 42
Mattathias, 19
Messiah, 54
Mishnah, 18
moral norms, 91, 93
Mosaic covenant, 4, 39, 75, 84, 85–86, 93, 123
Moses, 9, 39, 80
motive, 76
murder, 39, 89, 90

narcissism, 49, 90, 108
neighbors, 89
neutrality, 132
new age, 36, 47, 90, 124
new covenant, 90, 92
new creation, 32–36, 37, 134
new exodus, 38–39
new perspective on Paul, 76, 78, 79, 82, 97
noncircularity, 126, 127, 130

obedience
  of Christ, 55, 67

GENERAL INDEX 149

and covenant love, 128
and eternal life, 129
to the law, 18, 79
and legalism, 76
in Mosaic covenant, 86
as perfect, 71, 79–81
objective genitive, 64, 65
old age, 36
old covenant, 33, 80, 87
Old Testament
  circumcision in, 9
  covenant promises in, 31, 32
  eschatological work of the Spirit in, 37
  justification in, 71
  prophecy in, 31
  prophets in, 21
  sacrifices in, 80
  works in, 80
opponents, 3–13

paganism, 9, 84
Palestinian Judaism, 76
parable of the Pharisee and tax collector, 135
paradox, 92
Passover, 72
patience, 115
Paul
  apostolic authority of, 5–6, 15
  as genuine apostle, 3
  as persecutor of the church, 19
  sufferings of, 50
Pauline gospel, 6, 27, 123
peace, 115
penal substitution, 53
people, pleasing of, 17
people of God, 12, 98–103
perfect obedience, 71, 79–81
persecution, 25, 50, 105
Peter, 23, 24, 25–27, 42, 103–6
Pharisees, 4, 8
Philo of Alexandria, 11, 129–30, 132
Phinehas, 19
piety, 49, 117
Pilate, Pontius, 44

"pillars," of the church, 24, 25, 107
pistis Christou, 64
polarity, 42–43
predestination, 128
present age, 34, 48
pride, 116, 117, 135
priority, 126
promises, 86
prophecy, 38
prophets, calling of, 21
Protestants, 77, 130, 132, 135
Pseudo-Philo, 129, 130, 131, 133
Ptolemies, 40
purity laws, 78, 105

Qumran Hodayot, 129, 130, 131, 133

ransom, 42, 72
reaping, 119, 120
reciprocity, 126
reconciliation, 58
redemption, 42, 43, 52, 58, 71, 72
redemptive history, 66, 88
Reformation, 69, 77, 133
restoration, 116–17
resurrection, 32–33, 44
revelation, 17, 20
reward, 118, 120
righteousness, 44, 48, 57, 59–63, 68, 70, 111, 124, 135
Roman Catholics, 132–33
Rosner, Brian, 91

Sabbath, 11, 78
sacrifices, 54, 80–81
salvation, 49, 54, 58, 69
salvation history, 66
same-sex relationships, 102
sanctification, 58
Sanders, E. P., 76–77, 128, 131, 132, 136
Satan, 34, 51
Scripture, inspiration of, 4
Second Temple Judaism, 10, 11, 41, 53, 76, 77, 128, 129–31, 136
Seleucids, 40

self-absorbed, 90, 108
self-deceit, 120
self-exaltation, 85
self-examination, 117–18
sexual sin, 113
sin
   and death, 50
   as deceptive, 117
   dominion of, 53
   and the law, 82–83
   power of, 112
   slavery to, 52
singularity, 126, 127, 128, 130
slander, 114
slavery, 39–43, 45, 52, 53, 84, 87, 101, 102
snakes, 116
social agendas, 109
social class, 43, 100–103, 124
social implications, 103–8, 109, 116
social sins, 114
Solomon, 39, 59
sorcery, 113
soteriology, 57, 63–64, 103
sowing, 119, 120
stealing, 39, 81–82, 89, 90
subjective-genitive reading, 64–65, 66, 67
substitution, 53
suffering, 50
superabundance, 126, 127, 130
supernatural revelation, 20
Syrian Antioch, 4, 70

table fellowship, 103, 105–6
teaching, 102, 119
temptation, 117, 120
Timothy, 23–24
Titus, 7, 23–24, 26, 106–7
twelve, 24, 25, 27

unbelievers, 71, 88, 121
uncircumcision, 8, 35, 133–34
unclean food, 105
unity, 97, 107, 108–9

VanLandingham, Chris, 129

walking metaphor, 112
Western culture, 16, 126
"whole law," 48, 89, 92
widows, 121
wilderness generation, 9
wild parties, 114
wisdom, 91
Wisdom of Solomon, 129, 131, 132
wives, 102, 114
works of the flesh, 111, 113–15
works of the law, 61, 75–76, 78–79, 81, 82, 133–34
works righteousness, 76, 77, 127, 133–34, 135, 136
Wright, N. T., 40–41, 57–58, 63–64, 77–78

zeal, 19–20
Zipporah, 9

Scripture and Ancient Sources Index

Genesis
12:1–3........41
17:6–8........41
17:9............8
17:9–14......7–8, 9, 97
17:10..........8
17:11..........8
17:14..........8
18:18..........41
22:17–18......41
26:5............86
49:17..........116

Exodus
3:8 LXX......33
4:24–26......9
6:6.............52
15:13..........52
18:4 LXX.....33
18:8 LXX.....33
18:9 LXX.....33
18:10 LXX...33

Leviticus
11...............104
12:3............9, 12

Numbers
21:6............116
21:8............116
21:9............116
25:6–13......19

Deuteronomy
7:8.............52
8:15............116
9:26............52
10:16..........11
13:5............52
14...............104
15:15..........52
21:8............52
21:23..........53
24:18..........52
25:1............59
25:3............50
27:26..........79
28:58..........79
30:6............11

Joshua
5:2–9..........9

1 Kings
8:32............59
8:46............80
18:40..........19
19:10..........19
19:14..........19

2 Chronicles
6:23............59

Ezra
9:8.............40
9:9.............40

Job
14:1 55
15:14 55
25:4 54
33:32 59

Proverbs
20:9 80

Ecclesiastes
7:20 80
10:8 116
10:11 116

Isaiah
1:17 59
11:15–16 52
25:8 33
26:19 33
31:5 LXX 34
32:14 37
32:15–18 37
35:9 71
40:2 52
40:3–11 52
41:14 71
42:16 52
42:17 52
42:20 52
42:24–25 52
43:1 71
43:2 52
43:5–7 52
43:9 60
43:14 71
43:16–19 52
43:22–24 52
43:26 60
44:3 38
44:5 38
44:22 71
44:23 71
44:24 71
51:11 71
52:3 71
53:5 71
53:6 72
53:8 72
53:10 72
53:11 72
53:12 72
60:16 LXX 34
62:12 71
63:4 71
63:9 71
65:17 .... 34, 36
65:18–19 36
66:1 36
66:7–11 36
66:22 34–35

Jeremiah
1:5 21
4:4 11
8:17 116

Ezekiel
34:27 LXX 34
36 38
36:24 38
36:25 39
36:26 39
36:27 39
37:1–14 33

Daniel
12:2–3 33

Joel
2:28 38
2:28–32 38

Amos
5:19 116
9:3 116

Matthew
11:11 55
12:32 34
13:39 34
13:40 34
13:49 34
24:3 34
28:20 34

Mark
1:15............54
7:19............104
10:30..........34
11:22..........65

Luke
14:27..........50
18:9–14........135
18:30..........34
20:35..........34

John
16:2............20
17..............107
19:17..........50

Acts
4:21............61
9................17
9:1–2..........19
9:4..............19
9:13–14........19
10:1–11:18...104
11:27–30......106
13–14..........25, 105
13:28..........61
13:47..........21n5
15..............4, 106
15:1............4, 8, 12
15:5............4, 12
16..............23
16:1............23–24
16:3............23–24
22..............17
22:3............18, 19
22:4–5........19
22:7–8........19
22:19–20......19
23:9............61
23:29..........61
24:5............61
24:12..........61
24:20..........61
26..............17
26:5............18
26:9–11........19

Romans
1:1..............5
1:18–3:20.....81
1:25............113
1:26–27........102
2:1–3..........81
2:5–11..........81
2:12–13........81
2:13............60
2:17–24........81
2:25–29........82
2:28–29........11
3:4..............60
3:9–18..........82
3:20............81
3:22............66, 67
3:27–4:5......135
3:27–4:25.....57
3:28............81
4................134
4:1..............61
4:4–5..........135
5:1..............43
5:9..............43
5:12–14........36
5:18–19........67
5:20............83
6:14–15........88
7................112
7:4..............51
7:5–25..........50
7:14–25........112
8:15............55
8:23............55
8:33............60
9–11............100
9:4..............55
9:30–10:8.....135
10:3............135
10:4............86
10:9–14........67
12:2............34
12:7–8..........119
12:9–21........114
13:8–10........89, 114
13:10..........90

1 Corinthians

1:1 5
1:20 34
2:6 34
2:8 34
3:18 34
4:2 61
4:4 60
6:9 102
6:11 43
7:21 102
7:31 34
8:1–3 114
9:1–2 17
9:1–14 119
9:11 119
9:15–16 118
9:19–23 ...... 26n11
9:21 92
10:11 .... 34, 54
12:28 119
13:1–13 114
14:33–36 102
15:1–11 ...... 25, 26
15:5 25
15:7 25
15:8–9 5
15:9 19
15:15 61
15:24–28 34
15:56 50–51
16:15–16 119

2 Corinthians

1:1 5
1:14 118
4:4 34
5:17 35
9:6 119
9:10 119
11:24 50
12:20 61

Galatians

1–2 .... 5, 15, 27
1:1 .... 5, 32, 34
1:1–5 48
1:2 107
1:4 .... 33, 34, 36, 48, 49, 72
1:6–9 16
1:7 6
1:8 16
1:8–9 52
1:10 .... 5, 17
1:11 .... 6, 17
1:12 17
1:13 19
1:13–14 ...... 18, 20
1:14 .... 19, 20
1:15 21
1:15–17 20
1:16–17 21
1:18–24 21
1:20 21
1:21–24 22
2:1–2 22
2:1–10 .... 26, 27, 106, 107
2:3 .... 23, 24, 106
2:3–5 .... 7, 23, 26, 42, 106–7
2:4 .... 23, 42
2:5 .... xi, 3, 23, 42
2:6 24
2:6–10 24
2:7 24
2:7–9 24
2:9 24
2:11–14 ...... 27, 42, 51, 78, 103, 105, 107, 109
2:11–21 25
2:14 .... xi, 3, 25, 26, 42, 70, 105, 106
2:15–21 ...... 26, 70
2:16 .... 12, 43, 61, 66, 67, 68, 75, 78
2:16–17 62
2:17 .... 44, 61
2:19 .... 12, 33, 42, 50, 70
2:19–20 ...... 42, 50, 70
2:19–21 70
2:20 .... 21n5, 33, 35, 51, 68, 69
2:21 .... 12, 47, 48, 54, 62, 70, 79, 80

3	100
3:1	51
3:1–5	51
3:1–9	134
3:2	12, 37, 51, 62, 69, 75, 78
3:3	36, 37, 69
3:5	12, 37, 51, 62, 69, 75, 78
3:6	62, 67, 68
3:6–7	68
3:6–9	41
3:6–14	67
3:7	67, 68
3:7–9	97
3:8	43, 61, 62, 68
3:9	68
3:10	41, 68, 71, 75, 79, 81, 88
3:10–12	12
3:10–14	68, 71
3:11	42, 43, 61, 62, 63–64, 68, 71, 79
3:12	68, 71, 134
3:13	42, 52, 53, 71, 72, 80
3:14	38, 41, 68
3:15–18	85
3:16	41, 86, 98
3:17	12
3:19	12, 82, 86
3:20	39
3:21	12, 62, 64
3:21–23	83
3:22	41, 66, 88
3:23	12, 41, 66, 88
3:23–25	66, 86
3:24	44, 61, 87
3:25	41, 66, 87, 88
3:26	98
3:27	101
3:28	42, 100
4:1	72, 87
4:1–7	87
4:2	54, 88
4:3	41, 55, 72, 84, 88
4:4	12, 41, 42, 54, 88
4:4–5	42, 52, 55, 72, 88
4:5	42, 52, 88
4:7	42
4:9	84
4:10	12
4:12–20	108
4:14	108
4:16	108
4:19	108
4:21	12, 88
4:21–31	98
4:21–5:1	84
4:22–26	41
4:26	35
4:29	37
4:29–5:1	41
5:2–4	7, 55
5:3	12, 47, 48, 89
5:4	12, 44, 61, 63
5:5	44, 63
5:6	35, 114, 133
5:10	6, 119
5:11	5, 17, 49
5:13–14	114
5:13–6:10	111
5:14	12, 39, 75, 89, 92
5:15	116
5:16	112, 121
5:16–18	36
5:17	34, 112
5:18	41, 83, 88, 112
5:19	113
5:19–21	113
5:19–23	113
5:20	113
5:20–21	114
5:21	111, 114
5:22	37
5:23	12, 90, 115, 117
5:25	37, 115
5:25–26	115
5:26	117
6:1	116
6:1–10	116
6:2	39, 75, 91, 92, 119
6:3	117
6:4	117, 119
6:5	118, 119
6:6	119

6:6–10.........119
6:7..............120
6:8..............37, 120
6:9..............120
6:10............119, 121
6:11–18.......99
6:12............49, 134
6:12–13.......6, 49
6:12–14.......49
6:13............12, 85
6:14............118
6:14............35, 49, 70
6:15............32, 34, 35, 49, 133
6:15–16.......134
6:16............38, 98
6:17............49
6:18............107

Ephesians
1:1..............5
1:5..............55
1:10............54
1:15............67
1:21............34
2:2..............34
2:7..............34
2:8–10.........135
2:11–22.......78
2:20............24
4:11............119
5:2..............115
5:22–33.......102
5:25–29.......114
6:5–9..........102

Philippians
1:1..............119
1:29............67
2:6–8..........67
2:12–13.......118
2:16............118
3:2–3..........11
3:2–11........57
3:5..............9, 18
3:6..............19
3:8..............65
3:9..............61, 66

Colossians
1:1..............5
1:4..............67
2:5..............67
2:11–12.......11
3:4..............69
3:14............114
3:18–19.......102
3:19............114
3:22–4:1......102
4:5..............121

1 Thessalonians
1:3..............65
2:19............118
5:12–13.......119

2 Thessalonians
3:5..............115

1 Timothy
1:1..............5
1:5..............115
1:9..............102
1:12–16.......5
1:13............19
2:11–14.......102
3:7..............119
3:16............44, 61
5:3–16.........121
5:17............119
5:17–18.......119
6:17............34

2 Timothy
1:1..............5
1:9..............135
1:18............61
2:13............67
4:10............34

Titus
1:1..............5
1:5–9..........119
2:5..............102
2:12............34
3:5..............135

Philemon
5 67

Hebrews
12:22 36

1 Peter
1:7 61

2 Peter
3:10 61
3:14 61

Revelation
2:2 61
3:12 36
3:17 49
14:5 61
20:15 61
21:2 36
21:10 36

DEUTEROCANON-ICAL WORKS
Sirach
21:2 116
45:5 18

1 Maccabees
1:15 9
1:41–50 9
1:60–61 10
2:24–26 19
2:50 19
2:54 19
2:58 19

2 Maccabees
2:21 18
6:10 10
8:1 18
14:38 18

4 Maccabees
4:25 10
4:26 18

OLD TESTAMENT PSEUDEPIGRAPHA
1 Enoch
71:15 34

4 Ezra
4:27 34
7:12–13 34
7:50 34
7:113–14 34
8:1 34
14:30 18

2 Baruch
4:2 36
14:13 34
15:8 34
44:8–15 34

Jubilees
15:12 9
15:25 10
15:26 10

Psalms of Solomon
17–18 41

DEAD SEA SCROLLS
Pesher Habakkuk (1QpHab)
5.7–8 34

Nahum Commentary (4QpNah)
5–8 53

Temple Scroll (11QTemple)
64.6–13 53

Damascus Document (CD)
6.10–11 34
6.14 34
12.23 34

PHILO
On the Migration of Abraham
89–93 11

On the Special Laws
1:6..............11
1:305 11

JOSEPHUS
Antiquities of the Jews
1:192 10
7:21 55

16:382..........55
20:34–42......10
20:43–46 10

MISHNAH
'Abot
2:7...............18
6:7...............18

New Testament Theology

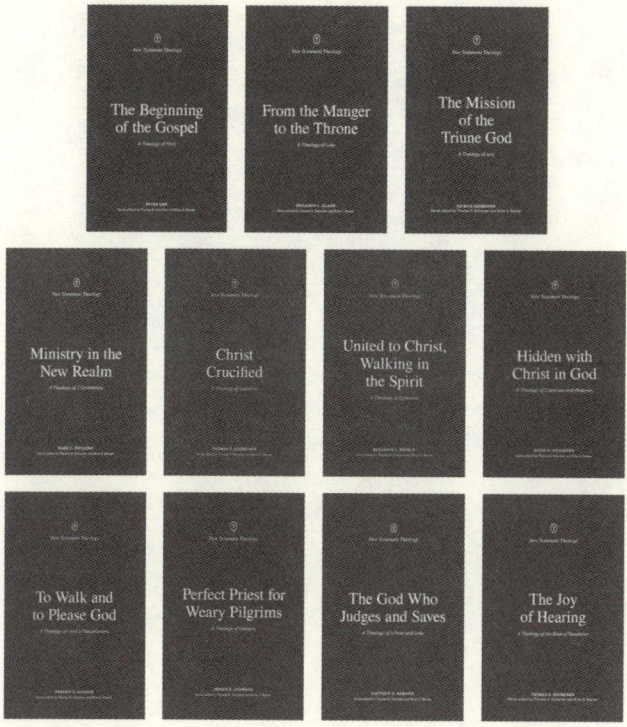

Edited by Thomas R. Schreiner and Brian S. Rosner, this series presents clear, scholarly overviews of the main theological themes of each book of the New Testament, examining what they reveal about God and his relation to the world in the context of the overarching biblical narrative.

For more information, visit **crossway.org**.